W9-BXD-489

Economic Contractions in the United States: A Failure of Government

By

Charles K. Rowley* and Nathanael Smith**

*Duncan Black Professor of Economics
George Mason University
and
General Director
The Locke Institute
crowley@gmu.edu

**Research Assistant in Economics
George Mason University
and
Senior Research Fellow
The Locke Institute
nathan_smith@ksg03.harvard.edu

The Locke Institute © 2009, in association with the Institute of Economic Affairs

First published in the United States in 2009 by

The Locke Institute
5188 Dungannon Road
Fairfax, Virginia 22030
www.thelockeinstitute.org

In association with the Institute of Economic Affairs

The mission of The Locke Institute is to promote the principles of limited government, individual liberty, private property, and the rule of law.

The mission of the Institute of Economic Affairs is to improve public understanding of the fundamental institutions of a free society, by analyzing and expounding the role of markets in solving economic and social problems.

ISBN 978-0-255-36642-7

Printed and bound in the United States by
Fairfax Printing
E-mail: printers@cox.net

CONTENTS

Contents

Figures

Acknowledgements

This project was organized and completed through the auspices of The Locke Institute in Fairfax, Virginia*, in association with the Institute of Economic Affairs in London, England**. The Locke Institute acknowledges with deep gratitude the financial support of the following individuals and foundations, without whose generosity we could not successfully have completed this monograph: The Institute of Economic Affairs; James T. Bennett; Robert S. Elgin; Gordon Tullock; The Chase Foundation of Virginia; and the Sunmark Foundation. Charles K. Rowley is grateful to the Department of Economics at George Mason University for honoring him with, and funding for him, the Duncan Black Chair in Economics. Nathanael Smith is grateful to the Department of Economics at George Mason University for funding his position as Research Assistant to Professor Rowley, and to The Locke Institute for his position as Senior Research Fellow. The Locke Institute is particularly indebted to Philip Booth, Editorial Director of the Institute of Economic Affairs, both for the intellectual support, and for the technical assistance, that he has generously provided at every stage in this project. The Institute also thanks Michael Perrott for superb proof reading.

*The Locke Institute
5188 Dungannon Road
Fairfax, Virginia 22030
USA
Tel: (703) 934-6934
Website: www.TheLockeInstitute.org
Email: crowley@gmu.edu
www.thelockeinstitute.org

**The Institute of Economic Affairs
2 Lord North Street
Westminster
London SW1P 3LB
England
Tel: 020 7799 8900
Email: iea@iea.org.uk
www.iea.org.uk

Preface for the Institute of Economic Affairs

T he IEA has decided to join with the Locke Institute in publishing this monograph because of the important lessons it contains regarding the financial crash of 2008 and the Great Depression of the 1930s. These lessons are ignored at our peril.

The US context for the current problems in the UK is important. Although UK banks clearly made bad business decisions, much of their bad debt originates from the purchase of US securitisation issues. The commentariat in the UK and the US is responding to the crisis by calling for more financial regulation and an end to the so-called laissez-faire capitalism that is said to have given rise to these financial innovations.

Yet, it is odd that they should do so unless they are blinkered by their own ideologies. It was a US monetary boom that fed an asset price boom and encouraged investors to under-price risk. It was the operation of monetary policy over a long period that led market participants to believe that a fall in the stock market would be cushioned by a fall in interest rates. The US government and its agencies were at the heart of the development of securitisation and also encouraged it through their tax and regulatory systems. US policy, over a generation, encouraged the "bail-out" mentality which, when combined with limited liability, is bound to lead to more and more recklessness in the management of financial institutions. Furthermore, US regulation encouraged the lending to poor risks that underlies so many of the toxic securities. Whether the commentariat is right in pointing the finger at unethical bankers and structural failings in markets is largely irrelevant. The US government – and its agencies – were encouraging, if not causing, the trends in financial markets that led to the crash of 2008. The government has shown that it is not in a position to correct what some call "market failure" and thus the appropriate regulatory response must be to restore the incentives that will ensure market discipline is effective.

This is not the main subject of the monograph by Charles Rowley and Nathanael Smith. But it is an important backdrop. Rowley and Smith show how the Great Depression – almost certainly caused by incompetent monetary policy managed by a Federal government body – was not only blamed on the market (like our own financial crash) but was used as an excuse to change the face of the US in a socialist direction. The US faces this threat again today.

In the wake of the Great Depression, Hoover raised tariffs and enacted legislation that kept wages artificially high. Roosevelt raised the top rate of tax to 79% and then to 90% in 1940. He established Planning Boards and led a shift of power from the states to the Federal government and from the Congress to the executive. Importantly, many of these changes lasted decades or became irreversible. These changes happened because it was believed by many in the establishment that the depression was caused by the market and could be resolved by various forms of socialism.

Thus this expansion of socialism was based on a fallacy. It also led to disastrous results as the US had arguably the deepest and longest-lasting depression of all the major industrial countries in the 1930s. Higher taxes, planning and regulation stifled the entrepreneurial initiative that should have been at the heart of economic recovery; government spending and investment crowded out much needed private spending and investment.

In the years prior to the crash of 2008, President George W. Bush was indulging in old-fashioned crude Keynesianism at a financial level – with disastrous long-run effects. As the authors put it:

> Tax cuts and deficit spending, M2 money supply growth, and low interest rates, made the period 2001 through 2007 the most expansionary economic policy environment in the United States since the 1970s. The Bush administration, the GOP-majority Congress, and the Greenspan Federal Reserve were, in effect if not in name, engaged in a great Keynesian experiment. And in the short run, it appeared to succeed.

And, with the election of the new President, the failure of crude Keynesianism has been followed by proposals to take government intervention in the economy to ever-greater levels. Obama is following the path trodden by Roosevelt, but with the additional twist that his starting point is one of much greater government intervention in the economy: this is partly because of the permanence of Roosevelt's reforms of 70 years ago and also because of expansion of government intervention under George W. Bush. Indeed, Rowley and Smith suggest that

Obama's interventions threaten the rule of law and the primacy of property rights.

This monograph by Rowley and Smith is important for the debate in the UK – and particularly important for the audience that the IEA tries to reach. A false understanding of the Great Depression, its causes and its aftermath is embedded in UK political discourse – even in intellectual circles. There is a danger that a false understanding of the causes of the crash of 2008, and the scale of government intervention that preceded it, will also become embedded. If that happens, then it will be that much more difficult to win the argument for the free economy.

But the authors go further than providing an historical account and critique. They propose a series of interesting and radical policy reforms which, at the same time, are within the realms of the politically possible – assuming, of course, that we have politicians with sufficient vision to implement them. Not all the proposals will obtain agreement from all supporters of the free market. Those relating to the conduct of monetary policy will be particularly controversial, but they should all form part of a vibrant debate amongst supporters of a free economy who come from different theoretical schools.

All supporters of a free economy will be in agreement though that we should not surrender intellectual ground to those who suggest that the Great Depression was caused by free market forces, that George W. Bush allowed unfettered market forces to prevail and that the crash of 2008 was caused by deregulation. Essentially this is an argument about education in recent economic history and the IEA is pleased to be associated with publishing Charles Rowley and Nathanael Smith's monograph in order that this process of education is advanced.

Philip Booth
Editorial and Programme Director, Institute of Economic Affairs;
Professor of Insurance and Risk Management; Cass Business School, City University, London, UK.
June 2009

The Authors

CHARLES K. ROWLEY

C harles Rowley was born in Southampton, England in 1939. He was educated at the University of Nottingham where he obtained a First Class Honours Degree in Economics in 1960 and a Ph. D. in Economics in 1964. He taught at the Universities of Nottingham, Kent, York and Newcastle upon Tyne and held summer fellowships in the Center for Socio-Legal Studies at Wolfson College, Oxford before migrating to the United States in January 1984 to join the Center for Study of Public Choice at George Mason University.

Dr. Rowley has written and edited some 40 books and some 200 scholarly papers in the fields of industrial organization, public choice, welfare economics, international trade and law-and-economics. His work consistently emphasizes the importance of private property rights, limited government and the rule of law as the basis for a free and prosperous society. Among his recent books are *The Right to Justice* (1992), *Property Rights and the Limits of Democracy* (edited 1993), *Trade Protection in the United States* (with Willem Thorbecke and Richard Wagner) (1995), *The Political Economy of the Minimal State* (edited 1996) and *Classical Liberalism and Civil Society* (edited 1997). He also edited *Public Choice Theory* (three volumes 1993), *Social Choice Theory* (three volumes 1993), *The Economics of Budget Deficits* (two volumes, with William F. Shughart, II and Robert D. Tollison, 2002), *The Encyclopedia of Public Choice* (two volumes, with Friedrich Schneider, 2004), and *The Origins of Law and Economics: Essays by the Founding Fathers* (with Francesco Parisi, 2005). Most recently, he has edited, with introductions, in ten volumes, *The Selected Works of Gordon Tullock* (2004-6).

Dr. Rowley was a Founding Editor, 1980-1986, of *The International Review of Law and Economics* and served as Joint Editor of *Public Choice* between 1990 and 2007. He is Duncan Black Professor of Economics at George Mason University, General Director of the Program in Economics, Politics and the Law in the James Buchanan Center for Political Economy, and General Director of *The Locke Institute*, an independent non-profit educational foundation located in Fairfax, Virginia and dedicated to the advancement of a classical liberal political economy.

NATHANAEL SMITH

Nathanael Smith is currently studying for a Doctoral Degree in Economics at George Mason University. He is a Senior Research Fellow at The Locke Institute in Fairfax, Virginia. He obtained a Bachelor's Degree in History and Economics from Notre Dame University and a Master's Degree in Public Administration and International Development from Harvard University. He worked as an analyst at the World Bank between October 2003 and July 2004, as a fiscal policy research analyst at The Cato Institute between August 2004 and July 2005, and as a consultant at the World Bank between August 2005 and January 2008. He has published a number of short articles in TCS Daily and a co-authored scholarly paper on Islam and Democracy (with Charles Rowley) in the June 2009 Issue of *Public Choice*.

In Memory of

Ralph Harris and Arthur Seldon
The Founding Fathers of the Institute of Economic Affairs

They dedicated their lives both to rolling back the state
and to promoting *laissez-faire* capitalism

Frontispiece

A comprehensive and coherent assessment of the current economic contraction, one that largely rebuts attribution of failure to capitalism or the market. The targets become the practicing politicians of all parties, whose cumulative mistakes have now hurt us all. We have learned some things from comparable experiences of the 1930s' Great Depression, perhaps enough to reduce the severity of the current contraction. But we have made no progress toward putting limits on political leaders, who act out their natural proclivities without any basic understanding of what makes capitalism work.

James M. Buchanan
Nobel Laureate in Economic Sciences, 1986

Foreword

By William F. Shughart II*

I t is now conventional to draw parallels between the sharp recession into which the United States and most of Europe plunged at the end of 2007 and the Great Depression of 1929–1945. The two events surely have much in common. Both were preceded by excessively loose monetary policies that fueled speculative asset bubbles – in the prices of real estate during the late 20th and early 21st centuries and in the market values of publicly traded equities during the Roaring Twenties. Both triggered epic responses from central governments worldwide after the bubbles inevitably burst, financial institutions collapsed, investors and businesses retrenched and unemployment spiked. Financed primarily by borrowing and informed by a fatal Keynesian conceit that governmental intervention can soften, indeed circumvent, painful but purgative market corrections, the Great Depression gave birth in America to Herbert Hoover's Reconstruction Finance Corporation and to Franklin D. Roosevelt's New Deal. Fiscal "stimulus" on a much larger scale, the Troubled Asset Relief Program, intended to clear balance sheets of toxic mortgage-backed securities and similarly worthless paper claims, and taxpayer-financed bailouts of banks, insurers, automobile manufacturers and other privately owned companies deemed too big to fail because of the perils of "systemic risk" are the accepted policy prescriptions for reversing today's economic decline.

But except for the warrants they supplied for unprecedented growth in the public sectors' size and scope, the comparisons between now and then are overwrought. By the time FDR moved into the White House in March 1933, thousands of banks had failed, US Gross Domestic Product had fallen by one-third and one in four Americans was out of work. By way of contrast, GDP has declined at an annualized rate of roughly 6.6% since December 2007 and the US unemployment rate stands, in spring 2009, at just under 9%. Those numbers unquestionably are cause for concern, but not for media-inspired panic. The crisis of the present day may deepen, of course; as of this writing, however, the economic data hardly justify the $3 trillion (or more) already committed by presidents George W. Bush and Barack Obama to a set of programs hopefully mimicking their collective hero FDR's triple goal of "relief, recovery and reform".

Nevertheless, as documented in this insightful monograph by Charles Rowley and Nathanael Smith, the Great Depression teaches important lessons about

xv

today's economy. Those lessons do not necessarily apply to the proximate causes of economic recession or depression in general, however. After all, economists have not 80 years on reached consensus as to whether the collapse that followed the stock market crash of October 1929 represented a failure of monetary policy, of fiscal policy, of international trade policy, or was instead caused by breakdowns in credit markets or in consumer confidence and business expectations. Complex events normally are not susceptible to simple explanation.

The key truth emphasized in the monograph at hand is that people have more to fear from governmental responses to economic crisis than from crisis itself. It is indisputable that the policies of the New Deal prolonged and deepened a downturn in business activity that otherwise likely would have been sharper, but briefer, as had been the experiences in all previous recessions. Despite all the legislative activity of FDR's famous First Hundred Days and of their nearly decade-long sequel, the US unemployment rate did not fall into the range of single digits until America had declared war on Japan on December 8, 1941, and Adolph Hitler soon thereafter foolishly had declared war on the United States. US GDP in real terms did not return to its 1929 level until Dwight Eisenhower was midway through his first term in office.

The Second World War may have solved the global unemployment problem but, as Robert Higgs has shown, it did not by any means restore prosperity. Conscription into the armed forces of millions of men, the shifting under a regime of war socialism of scarce resources into the production of armaments, and the rationing of rubber, sugar, gasoline and other consumer goods hardly were recipes either for liberty or affluence. Economic growth returned to pre-1929 trajectory only when, after Allied victory over the Axis powers in 1945 and, contra Keynes and Cambridge, Washington had cut it its war-related expenditures sharply, lowered personal and corporate income tax rates and reduced its war-time budget deficits. Such evidence flies in the face of the conclusions of Paul Krugman, Christina Romer, Lawrence Summers and other contemporary philosopher-kings (and queens), who argue that the New Deal failed to turn the economy around simply because it was too timid.

The policies of the New Deal, aimed at propping up prices and wages at a time when markets were calling for them to fall, and at restricting output when the economy was in the midst of a staggering freefall in the production of goods and services, short-circuited the therapeutic operation of unfettered market forces. More seriously, FDR's program of policy experimentation – guided by his overarching philosophy of trying something and, if that didn't work, of trying something else – fostered a climate of uncertainly that chilled business's incentives to invest in new plant and equipment and to begin hiring again. What was needed, then as now, was a policy stance that obeyed the Hippocratic Oath, which instructs physicians, first, to do no harm.

Rowley and Smith herein also summarize evidence that should not be too surprising – although it may well be so to the majority voting in November 2008 in favor of change they could believe in – that political influence shaped the distribution of New Deal spending. FDR has been accused of many things, but political naïveté is not one of them. He grasped early on that solidifying a supporting coalition comprised of blue-collar workers, farmers, big-city political machines, voters in key western swing-states, African-Americans and intellectuals, among others, was essential to his strategy for election to a second term in 1936. Federal largesse predictably flowed disproportionately from Washington to electorally critical states and special-interest groups, while the solidly Democratic South got short-shrift. That same vote motive seems to be in play in President Obama's first budget request, in the ending of his predecessor's post-9/11 tax cuts and in his support for labor unions, for single-payer (nationalized) healthcare, and for fuel-efficient vehicles, ethanol and other "green" policy initiatives.

Informed by the Virginia School of positive public choice analysis, *Economic Contractions in the United States* supplies timely and indispensable historical perspectives on the financial crisis that produced the economic recession of 2007 that still is underway. Rowley and Smith's monograph focuses attention on the salient fact that, like the Great Depression before it, the current recession is man-made. It resulted from the predictable responses of profit-seeking lenders to a sequence of public policies that supplied incentives for advancing money to borrowers who could not possibly afford to square their accounts unless the bets they (and their counterparty financial institutions) had made on continuously rising real estate prices paid off. Those bets generated handsome returns for quite some time, but the rents generally were squandered by homeowners by taking out second mortgages, cashing in their equity to finance current consumption spending. Lenders, likewise mesmerized by seemingly ever-rising collateral values – and anticipating, correctly as it turned out, that any capital losses could be shifted to the taxpayers, i.e., government-sponsored entities (GSEs), such as Fannie Mae, Freddie Mac and the Federal Housing Authority – willingly and rationally assumed more exposure to default risk.

Now that the chickens have come home to roost, what is to be done? In answering that important question, I can do no better than to recommend careful attention to chapters 5 and 6 of *Economic Contractions in the United States*, where the essential elements of a *laissez faire* program for recovery and reform ably are spelled out. At the end of the day, though, I am less sanguine than the authors about the prospects for substantive change along the lines they propose. I fear that many Americans, who have benefited greatly from free-market institutions, value government protection from downside risk more than they value opportunities to improve their standards of living. I hope that I am wrong. If so, it will be to Charles Rowley and Nathanael Smith that thanks are owed. If not, America is destined to become a simulacrum of France, overseen in the near term by an administration so profligate that his predecessor now looks like the fiscal conservative he claimed to be, and by a central bank that, under the chairmanship of Ben Bernanke, fatally has compromised its independence from the executive branch. The permanently larger public sector that in my judgment will be the chief legacy of the current recession augurs a US economy that will be much less resilient when the next crisis strikes, justifying demands for even more socialization.

* F.A.P. Barnard Distinguished Professor
  Department of Economics
  University of Mississippi

  Editor in Chief, *Public Choice*

  President-elect, Southern Economic Association

The Setting

Economic Contractions in the United States: A Failure of Government.

Charles K. Rowley and Nathanael Smith

"An impoverished vocabulary, rich only in euphemisms, calls what has happened to the economy in consequence of the collapse a 'recession'. We are well beyond that."

"Some conservatives believe that the depression is the result of unwise government policies. I believe it is a market failure."

Richard A. Posner (2009) *A Failure Of Capitalism: The Crisis Of '08 And The Descent Into Depression*, vi and xii.

"This land of such dear souls, this dear, dear land,
Dear for her reputation through the world,
Is now leased out, I die pronouncing it,
Like to a tenement or pelting farm:
(The United States), bound in with the triumphant sea,
Whose rocky shore beats back the envious siege
Of watery Neptune, is now bound in with shame,
With inky blots and rotten parchment bonds:
That (United States) that was wont to conquer others
Hath made a shameful conquest of itself."

William Shakespeare, *Richard II*, Act II, Sc.i
(with apologies to Sir John of Gaunt)

1
Introduction

F ree enterprise capitalism works as a wealth-creating process. Capitalism works better, in this respect, than any other economic system. The closer the economic system approaches to *laissez-faire*, the more powerful its wealth-creating impulse. That is the lesson of economics and of economic history since the late 18th century. Social market economies, in the sense of Old Europe, may have beneficial characteristics. But the last three decades in Western Europe have shown that significant, sustainable wealth-creation is not among those characteristics.

A comparison with France and Germany sheds an interesting light on the anti-capitalist rhetoric that has circulated in the past year of economic contraction in the United States. According to the OECD, Germany's GDP per capita in 2006 was $31,950; France's, $31,047; and that of the United States, $44,054. U.S. per capita GDP is 27 per cent higher than Germany's, 29 per cent higher than France's. The peak-to-trough drop in real incomes during the Great Depression of 1929-33 was 36 per cent. An "L-shaped" depression, involving continuing high unemployment and a decade or so of stagnant growth, is often cited as a worst-case scenario for the US economy's immediate future. Yet even if US per capita GDP was to fall by one-quarter, a collapse only slightly less severe than that of 1929-33, its economy would remain ahead of those of France and Germany, even in the unlikely event that the latter remain completely unaffected by the present adverse economic environment.

American liberals have long praised Continental Western Europe (as late as 1989, Nobel Laureate, Paul Samuelson actually praised the German Democratic Republic) as economic models that the United States should emulate. One might ask, then, why should the left regard a second Depression as something to be avoided? If France and Germany are really worth emulating, should not such liberals regard a fall in GDP on the scale of the Great Depression as a price worth paying for a European-style social market economy?

It is doubtful, however, whether a majority of Americans really want to trade the capitalist prosperity they have enjoyed for the past generation for the safety and stagnation of European-style social market economies. Rather, politicians and pundits are trying to convince Americans that it is possible to have *both* American-style prosperity and dynamism *and* European-Union-style social markets. Recent history suggests that this is a pipe-dream.

Business cycles (or business fluctuations as they are sometimes referred to) are normal features of a well-functioning capitalist system. Upturns in the cycle unleash entrepreneurial forces that create new products and services that both shape and cater to the changing tastes of consumers. Downturns, usually caused by the excessive expansion of the money supply in a fractionalized reserve banking system (Mises 1912, Hayek 1933, 1935), nevertheless play an indispensable role in cleansing out accumulated structural inefficiencies, just as forest fires contribute to the long-run health of a forest.

This periodic cyclical cleansing reinforces the process of "creative destruction" (Schumpeter 1942), whereby resources are moved from lower to higher valued uses in response to changes in consumer preferences and/or in technology. Only when business cycles are driven beyond their natural limits by inappropriate monetary policy does capitalism occasionally explode into hyper-inflation on the one hand, or into economic depression on the other hand. These outliers almost always represent a failure of government, not of *laissez-faire* capitalism. Such is the case today.

In a recent book, Richard Posner has unequivocally categorized the economic contraction that started in the United States in late 2007 as a *depression*, and has identified its cause primarily as a *failure of capitalism* (Posner 2009). By contrast, we suggest that the current economic recession, like the extended Great Depression of 1929-39, represents a *failure of government*, and of *state capitalism* that is its creation, certainly not a failure of *laissez-faire* capitalism.

We divide this monograph into seven chapters, including this introduction. Chapter 2 revisits in some depth the Great Depression and its aftershocks in order to determine what really went wrong. We reject the myth that conservative fiscal policies caused the collapse and that Keynesian fiscal policies pulled the US economy out of the Great Depression. Rather, excessively loose monetary policy was the cause of the stock market bubble that burst in 1929, while excessively tight monetary policy was the principal reason that a normal recession in 1929 turned into a deep depression. Later, a relaxation of monetary policy was the main reason for a brief and limited recovery after 1933. But FDR's interventionist policies and draconian tax increases delayed full economic recovery by several years by exacerbating a climate of pessimistic expectations that drove down private capital formation and household consumption to unprecedented lows.

Chapter 3 shifts attention to the two economic contractions that have occurred in the US during the first decade of the twenty-first century, that of 2001-2 and that of late 2007 onwards. We demonstrate that excessively loose monetary policies were prime causes of the stock market bubbles that burst in 2000 and in 2008 and of the housing bubble that burst in mid-2006, and that expansionist, Keynesian fiscal policies pursued by the Bush administration from 2001 onwards, though they helped to make the 2001 recession one of the mildest on record, did so at the cost of becoming the root cause of the 2008 financial crisis and economic contraction. Unfortunately, the newly-elected Obama administration, together with its Congressional allies, has chosen to double or triple Bush's Keynesian bets, trying to revive the economy by putting the government still further into debt through easy money, temporary tax cuts, and large increases in government spending. Moreover, there are troubling similarities between the emerging industrial policy of the newly-elected Obama administration and the disastrous industrial policies of FDR.

Chapter 4 outlines and challenges the hypothesis set out by a number of scholars and commentators of the 2008 financial crisis (including Posner 2009) that capitalism has failed in the United States. We distinguish between *laissez-faire* capitalism and state capitalism and demonstrate that the latter failed, not the former. State capitalism failed largely because of the state, though capitalists within the financial sector contributed to the failure through serious and widespread lapses in financial judgment and personal integrity.

Chapter 5 draws upon the experience of the Great Depression and the 2001-2009 economic experience to define a Virginia political economy program of policy reform designed to counter the current economic contraction and to restore the US economy to its New Economy rates of productivity growth evidenced throughout the period of the Great Moderation, but most especially during the 1990s.

Chapter 6 draws on cutting-edge contributions in public choice economics to explain why regulation failed to prevent the 2000-2006 housing-market bubble and the 2008 financial crisis that followed its bursting. Public choice theory also provides a framework for an incentive-compatible, rules-based regulatory framework designed to prevent the recurrence of such a financial crisis in the United States.

Chapter 7 summarizes the major conclusions derived from this monograph and re-emphasizes the need for a return to some form of politically feasible approximation to *laissez-faire* capitalism, as the best way to achieve sustainable economic growth.

The Virginia School of Political Economy (Rowley and Vachris 1996, Shughart 2004, Tollison 2004) shows why Keynesian economists set themselves too easy and too useless a task when they craft advice for politicians and bureaucrats as if the latter were Platonic philosopher-kings rather than fallible and often self-seeking careerists (Buchanan and Wagner 1978). The problem is not with particular politicians, but rather, that even if there is a sound case for Keynesian-style demand management in pure macroeconomic theory (which is questionable), it is, as Buchanan and Wagner argue, "misapplied... to the political institutions of a functioning democratic society." (Buchanan and Wagner 1977, 5).

To set the scene for our unfolding analysis we present a very simple model which illustrates the virtue of market-friendly policy rules, a model that captures the most ominous policy similarities between the years after 1929 and the 2008-9 policy responses to the present crisis. Consider the two-player game shown in **Figure 1**:

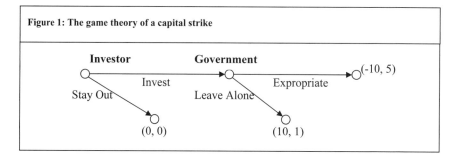

Figure 1: The game theory of a capital strike

In Figure 1, an Investor has two options: Invest or Stay Out. The Government then has two options: Expropriate, or Leave Alone. The payoffs are as shown, with the Investor's payoff first, the Government's payoff second. The game can be solved by backward induction. If play reaches the second node, and the Government gets to move, it is rational for the Government to play Expropriate. Foreseeing this, the Investor in his first move, will play Stay Out, and both players receive a zero payoff. But both would be better off if the Government could somehow pre-commit to play Leave Alone, in which case the Investor will select Invest and the payoffs would be ten for the Investor, one for the Government (which benefits from more tax revenues and employment if the Investor invests). The Virginia School argues the case for constitutional rules that enable Government to bind itself to the mast and resist the siren song of intervention.

Our proposals, some at least of which are designed to appeal to the median US voter to the extent possible, seek a path to restore and deepen the institutional foundations of capitalist prosperity and growth, including individual liberty, a level playing field for business, private property rights, limited government, and the rule of law. Unfortunately the political climate, in the wake of the November 2008 elections, is currently unfavorable to a pro-capitalist reform program.

Therefore, we await a favorable wind on which to set sail to reverse the currently pro-social market economy agendas of the Obama administration and the Democrat-controlled US Congress, in order to return the United States economy, as far as is feasible within the constraints of a contemporary United States constitutional republic, to *laissez-faire* capitalism.

2

The Great Depression and Its Aftershocks, 1929-1939: An Analytical History

T he great economic contraction in the United States began with a stock market crash. Stock prices had reached their peak on September 7th, 1929, when Standard and Poor's composite price index of 90 common stocks stood at 254. A decline over the following four weeks was intermittent and caused no panic. Indeed, after falling to 228 on October 4, the index rose to 245 on October 10. The subsequent decline degenerated into a panic on October 23. On October 24, Black Thursday, stockholders dumped large blocks of securities onto the market. On October 29, when the index fell to 162, some 16.5 million shares were traded, compared with little more than 4 million shares per day throughout the preceding month of September. Nonetheless, as of the end of 1930, the situation looked no worse than a normal business downturn. By the end of the year, historian John Steele Gordon reports that:

> By December stocks were moving upward, although on much reduced volume. By year's end, while many of the high-flying stocks had been savaged, some market sectors—such as airplane manufacturers, department stores, and steel companies—actually showed gains for the year. It was widely thought the crash had been only a severe correction for a much overbought market. In January 1930 the *New York Times* thought the biggest news story of 1929 had been Admiral Byrd's flight over the South Pole. (Gordon, 2004, 318)

Instead, the contraction became so severe that by July 1932, the Standard and Poor Index was valued only at 50, one fifth of its peak value, the Dow Jones Industrial Average fell from a peak value of 381 in September 1929 to a low value of 41 in July 1932, and stocks did not recover their nominal 1929[1] levels until November 1954 (Friedman and Schwartz 1963).

---

[1] Remember, however, that the Consumer Price Index was trending downwards through the Great Depression, implying that stock prices fell significantly less in real than in nominal terms.

Gross national product in nominal prices declined rapidly throughout the period 1929 to 1933: by 15 per cent from 1929-30, by 20 per cent from 1930 to 1931, by 27 per cent from 1931 to 1932, and by a further 5 per cent from 1932 to 1933. A rapid rate of decline in the general price level (deflation) implied that real gross national product declined somewhat less. All told, money income fell by 53 per cent and real income by 36 per cent over the four years of the great contraction. Aggregate real income in 1933 was below the level of 1916, even though the population had grown by 23 per cent. Per capita real income in 1933 was almost the same as it had been in the trough year of 1908, a quarter of a century earlier (Friedman and Schwartz 1963).

The rate of unemployment increased each year throughout the great contraction, from 3.2 per cent in 1929, to 8.9 per cent in 1930, to 16.3 per cent in 1931, to 24.1 per cent in 1932 and to a peak of 24.9 per cent in 1933. Thereafter, it remained stubbornly high, at 21.7 per cent in 1934, 20 per cent in 1935, 16.9 per cent in 1936, 14.3 per cent in 1937, 19 per cent in 1938 and 17.2 per cent in 1939. This situation was especially serious because the workforce was composed mainly of male heads of households only at this time. In such circumstances, at the trough of the contraction, one household out of four had no gainfully employed member. The great contraction did not erase advances in technology; rather it proceeded by idling men and machines (Friedman and Schwartz 1963).

There have been many recessions in US history but none came close to the severity of the Great Depression. Why was this particular downturn so catastrophic?

Economists do not agree about the primary cause of the initial 1929 downturn in stock prices and real output. Marxists argued that capitalism was doomed because of its inherent contradictions (at the trough of the depression, this was perhaps the dominant view within the US economics profession[2]). Some populists focused their attack on the alleged failure of the Gold Standard – the so-called Cross of Gold (Eichengreen 1992). Others (Schlesinger 1958) focused attention on alleged structural defects, notably malfeasance on the part of bankers and industrialists, incompetence of government officials, economic bubbles and the like (arguments that are recycling at the present time). No doubt each viewpoint had some justification within the economic climate of the 1930s.

---

[2] In this tradition, even Frank Knight, of the relatively free market department of economics at the University of Chicago, circulated a pamphlet during the 1930s entitled: The case for communism: from the standpoint of an ex-liberal (Samuels 1991, 57-108).

But a long list of major detrimental policies, some implemented during the 1920s, but most during the Hoover and the (first and second) Roosevelt administrations, account for so much damage to the economy that it is a stretch to attribute the crash to some inherent flaw in *laissez-faire* capitalism. The following is a partial list of these bad policies.

2.1. MONETARY POLICY: FIRST EASY MONEY, THEN DEFLATION

The most influential US economist at that time, Irving Fisher (1911, 1920), whose views would later influence Milton Friedman, argued convincingly that the predominant factor leading to the great contraction was the combination of excessive indebtedness with deflation (Fisher 1933). Fisher tied loose credit to over-indebtedness, which fueled speculation and asset bubbles. In 1929, United States non-federal debt was 164 per cent of gross domestic product (*The Economist*, February 14, 2009, 79). Mortgage debt was modest relative to home values, and home prices were not notably inflated, falling 24 per cent between 1929 and 1933, roughly in line with the fall in the Consumer Price Index.

Once the bubble burst, Fisher (1933) argued, debt liquidation and distress selling contributed to a fall in asset prices, a collapse in the net worth of companies, and a dramatic increase in the rate of bankruptcy. These, in turn, induced pessimism and a loss of confidence, among both investors and consumers. Deflation intensified the burden of debt, encouraged further hoarding, and thus exacerbated the reduction in output, trade and employment. The deflationary spiral was severe following the Great Crash in 1929 (http://shmoop.com/did-you-know/history/us.the-great-depression/statistics.html; Chantrill 2009).

In 1929, the Consumer Price Index (CPI) was stable. In 1930, the CPI fell by 2.53 per cent, in 1931, by 8.8 per cent, and, in 1932, by 10.31 per cent, all under the Hoover administration. In 1933, the CPI continued to fall, by 5.13 per cent. Then, it reversed course, increasing by 3.35 per cent in 1934, by 2.49 per cent in 1935, by 0.97 per cent in 1936, and by 3.61 per cent in 1937. In 1938 and 1939 deflation returned, with the CPI declining by 1.86 per cent and 1.42 per cent respectively, as the deflationary decade stumbled to its end. Real debt burdens shot up during the great economic contraction because they were denominated largely in nominal terms during a period of deflation and shrinking output.

It is worth noting that the general price level declined significantly, *pari passu* as the decline in the quantity of money, as classical theory correctly predicted, a fact sharply at odds with the emphasis on downward "price and wage stickiness" by Keynesian economists.

Keynesians traditionally attribute this deflationary spiral to a "liquidity trap," but Friedman and Schwarz (1963) argue persuasively that the great deflation can be fully explained by shrinkage of the M2 money supply. Monetary policy played a major role both in inducing and in lengthening the economic contraction. Fearing price inflation during a period of soaring industrial production and rising stock prices, the Federal Reserve began to sterilize inflows of gold into the United States in 1928.

The money supply (M2) began to level off in 1929, following a lengthy period of excessive expansion underwritten by the *Federal Reserve Bank of New York* under the powerful chairmanship of Benjamin Strong. By failing to counter the fall in M2 by restoring the quantity of high-powered money once bank failures became pandemic, a post-Benjamin Strong Federal Reserve System placed the United States economy into a several-year monetary refrigerator (http://www.shmoop.com/did-you-know/history/us/the-great-depression/statistics.html).

In 1929, M2 balances increased by 0.39 per cent, as the Federal Reserve Board intervened to reduce its rate of growth. In 1930, some 700 banks failed, mostly in rural communities, without attracting the attention of the Federal Reserve Board. M2 declined by 1.8 per cent. At the end of 1930, a major Jewish-owned bank that had served immigrants in New York, the *Bank of United States*, failed. This triggered a loss of depositor confidence.

In 1931, bank failures increased in earnest, many of them state-chartered banks outside the purview of the Federal Reserve Board. These failures, combined with money supply inaction on the part of the Federal Reserve Board, contracted the money supply. In 1931, M2 declined by 6.65 per cent and US cities began to issue scrip while individuals began to barter with each other.

In 1932, as bank failures mounted yet further, in a move reminiscent of the *Troubled Asset Repurchase Program* of 2008, and other government bailouts during the current crisis, President Hoover signed into law the *Reconstruction Finance Act* that created a *Reconstruction Finance Corporation* to loan federal dollars to banks, railroads and agricultural organizations. This notwithstanding, M2 spiraled downwards during 1932 by a momentous 15.55 per cent. By the time that Franklin Roosevelt assumed the Presidency, the banks in many states were closed. Even the Federal Reserve *Bank of New York* had closed its doors. The new administration moved swiftly, ramming a large volume of legislation through the Democrat-controlled Congress. Most notable, from the viewpoint of monetary policy, was the *Emergency Banking Relief Act* that took the United States off the Gold Exchange Standard and reopened the banks. Nevertheless, M2 continued on its downward path, declining by a further 10.62 per cent during 1933.

As Friedman and Schwartz (1963) note: "From the cyclical peak in August 1929 to the cyclical trough in March 1933, the stock of money fell by over a third. More than one-fifth of the commercial banks in the United States, holding nearly one-tenth of the volume of deposits at the beginning of the contraction, suspended operations because of financial difficulties." They conclude that "the monetary collapse was not the inescapable consequence of other forces, but rather a largely independent factor which exerted a powerful influence on the course of events." (Friedman and Schwartz 1963)

In any event, M2 recovered somewhat in 1934, increasing by 6.64 per cent. A more significant increase occurred in 1935, with M2 rising by 13.71 per cent. In the election year of 1936, M2 rose by 11.29 per cent and in 1937 by 5.06 per cent. In 1938, M2 slipped downwards by 0.37 per cent, but recovered in 1939 with an increase of 8.26 per cent. (http://www.shmoop.com/did-you-know/history/us/the-great-depression/statistics.html)

Christina Romer (1993) reports an increase in the monetary base of 52 per cent and in M1 of 49 per cent between April 1933 and April 1937, largely because the Treasury refused to sterilize the large inflows of gold from Europe. In this sense, the increased supply of money can be viewed as a policy decision, and not simply the endogenous reaction of the money multiplier (Parker 2009).

Friedman and Schwartz (1963) probably overreach in arguing that the Great Depression was caused almost entirely by monetary contraction. One problem is that the theoretical basis for believing that a monetary contraction could have such an enormous adverse impact on the real economy is weak. According to the quantity theory, as formalized by Irving Fisher (1911), changes in the quantity of money do not impact output at all in the long run (the classical dichotomy).

In the short run, changes in the quantity of money may impact output as a consequence of changes in the income velocity of circulation of money, but classical economists never contemplated an impact of money on output as significant as that implied by the Friedman-Schwarz hypothesis. Friedman's 1956 restatement of the quantity theory (Friedman 1956) did little to enhance the supposed output effect of changes in the supply of money. Friedman's portfolio theory - modeling the demand for money as a stable function of several variables - found strong empirical support. Subsequent theoretical advances (Friedman 1968, Gordon 1974) concerning changes in the money supply under adaptive expectations, predicted short-term real-output effects, but no long-term real-output effects.

The New Classical rational expectations (Lucas 1972) closed even that gap. Only monetary shocks could produce output effects, and the ability of the monetary authorities to surprise the system would erode as quickly as it was practiced. The New Keynesian rational expectations (De Long and Summers 1986, Summers 1988) predicted minor real output responses to anticipated as well as unanticipated changes in the supply of money, in the short-run, but not in the long-run, as part of a more general, but very weak, resuscitation of Keynesian economics.

So, even if the Federal Reserve Board can "push on a string"—that is, if the M2 money supply is really an output policy instrument at the Federal Reserve's disposal, a proposition that Keynes's "liquidity trap" hypothesis denies—there is no theoretical consensus whether or how an expansionary monetary policy throughout the lengthy period of the great contraction could have halted, much less have reversed the direction of, economic decline. To constitute a more adequate explanation of the Depression, the Friedman-Schwarz (1963) hypothesis needs to be combined with the "financial accelerator" idea of Ben Bernanke (1983).

2.2. BEN BERNANKE AND THE "FINANCIAL ACCELERATOR"

Ben Bernanke (1983, 2000) builds on the monetary hypothesis of Friedman and Schwartz (1963) to develop an alternative interpretation of the way in which the financial crisis affected output. His theory combines Fisher's (1933) argument concerning the economic effects of debt deflation with arguments concerning the impact of bank panics on the ability of financial markets to arbitrage the allocation of funds from lenders to borrowers. Bernanke's (1983) article is an important contribution in its own right; but it has a special importance because it has clearly informed the Federal Reserve's response to the financial crisis since Bernanke took over as Chairman of the Federal Reserve in 2006.

Bernanke (1983) outlines what is now called the "credit view". He argues that in normal circumstances an initial decline in the price level simply reallocates wealth from debtors to creditors, such as banks. Such adjustments do not impact the economy. However, when confronted by large shocks, deflation in asset prices forfeited to banks by debtor bankruptcies reduces the nominal value of assets on bank balance sheets. For a given level of bank liabilities, also denominated in nominal terms, this decline in the value of bank assets threatens insolvency.

In response, banks reallocate assets away from private loans in favor of government securities, thus rationing credit for some borrowers. Such rationing reduces investment and consumption expenditures in the macro-economy, which contributes further to the downward deflationary spiral. For such a downward spiral, a substantial build-up of debt must have occurred prior to the onset of economic contraction. In addition, deflation must have been partially unanticipated when the debt build-up occurred. These conditions were in place in the specific case of the great economic contraction (Fackler and Parker, 2001, Hamilton 1992, Evans and Wachtel 1993, Parker 2009). They apply to the 2008-2009 period as well.

Furthermore, the sequence of financial panics that occurred over the period 1929 to 1933 obstructed the credit allocation mechanism. Bernanke (1983) argues that the process of credit intermediation requires significant information gathering and sophisticated market mechanisms. Financial panics and debtor and business bankruptcies increase the real cost of such credit intermediation, adversely affecting households, farmers and small businesses. Evidence in support of this hypothesis for the period 1929 to 1933 is substantial (Bernanke 1983, Fackler and Parker 1994, 2001, Hamilton 1987, 1992).

2.3. TAXES AND SPENDING: WAS FISCAL RESPONSIBILITY A VICE?

Keynesian and New Keynesian macroeconomists today (though surely not New Classical macroeconomists, Real Business Cycle theorists, Austrian economists, and Virginia School economists) would probably agree that Herbert Hoover's initial efforts to balance the budget harmed the economy (Kindleberger 1973). The federal government's initial fiscal response was to maintain budget surpluses throughout 1929 and 1930, albeit at rates below 1 per cent of GDP. The top rate of income tax was held at 25 per cent. In 1931, the budget moved slightly into deficit (0.78 per cent of GDP), with the maximum income tax rate still holding at 25 per cent. Only in 1932 did the federal budget move sharply into deficit (6.81 per cent of GDP) even though the Hoover administration doubled all tax rates and hiked the maximum rate of income tax to 63 per cent.(http://www.shmoop.com/did-you-know/history/us/the-great-depression/statistics.html)

Running against Hoover in November 1932, Franklin Roosevelt criticized Hoover for running budget deficits. But once in office, the first Roosevelt administration ran a budget deficit of 7.98 per cent of GDP in 1933, which increased again in 1934 to 8.94 per cent and in 1935 fell back slightly to 5.46 per cent, while the top rate of income tax was held at 63 per cent.

In 1936, in a bid to sway the upcoming election, the Roosevelt administration soaked the better off with a hike in the top rate of income tax to 79 per cent, while increasing federal expenditures to states considered marginal for Electoral College votes (Shughart 2004). The budget deficit ran at 6.56 per cent of GDP. With the election won in a landslide, at the price of a second economic contraction, a shift to fiscal conservatism followed, under the second Roosevelt administration, with the budget deficit falling to 2.72 per cent of GDP in 1937, and again to 0.12 per cent of GDP in 1938. In 1939, with war in Europe under way, and the US re-arming, the budget deficit ticked up to 3.47 per cent of GDP. (http://www.shmoop.com/did-you-know/history/us/the-great-depression/statistics.html). Of course, during the Second World War, the US government ran enormous deficits.

From 1929 to 1945, there seems to be a strong positive correlation between government deficits and the performance of the economy. Thus, the economy declined sharply under the fiscally "responsible" Hoover, recovered tepidly in the first, deficit spending years of Roosevelt, plunged back into recession when the Roosevelt administration turned slightly fiscally conservative in 1937-38, then accelerated enormously during the huge deficit spending years of the Second World War. These experiences created in the economics profession a long-lasting bias in favor of fiscal policy as a tool of macroeconomic management. But there are two problems with this reasoning.

First, correlation is not causation, and there may have been other reasons for some of these developments, for example the decline of M2 during the Hoover years, the adverse supply-side effects of Roosevelt's tax hikes in 1936, and the re-legitimization of private profit-seeking business when the need to win the Second World War gave patriotic political cover to the protagonists of productivity after 1940. The deficit spending/growth correlation does not apply outside of the period, for example to the 1920s, 1970s, or 1990s.

Second, even if deficit spending does, under certain circumstances, provide a short-run economic boost, this is of little importance if it causes long-run damage to the economy. While some of the years between 1929 and 1945 were better than others, none of them were times of peace and prosperity such as America prefers and has often achieved, and which, in the fiscally responsible 1920s or 1990s, seemed merely normal.

In fact, private investment was feeble throughout the 1930s, which is consistent with the hypothesis that government deficits were crowding it out (Higgs 1987). Yet it may be the case that in the later Roosevelt years investor confidence had been so devastated by market turmoil, exorbitant taxes, the arbitrary and perverse interventions of the National Industrial Recovery Act (NIRA), shameless show trials of figures like Andrew Mellon and Sam Insull [3], anti-capitalist rhetoric, attempts to pack the US Supreme Court and, in general, the ruin of the economic constitution of the United States as it had existed until that time, that it was impossible for Roosevelt to make credible commitments not to expropriate private investors *ex post* and thereby to make it rational for those with capital to create enterprises and generate productive jobs (Reed 1981/2008, Couch and Shughart 1998).

2.4. MICROECONOMIC POLICIES

The Great Depression has generally been treated as a "macro" problem, but "micro" causes may be equally important. As mentioned before, in 1932 income tax rates were doubled and a 63 per cent top rate of income tax was imposed. The Revenue Act of 1932 also raised the corporate income tax rate by 15 per cent, and doubled the estate tax. For reasons later elucidated by supply-side economists like Arthur Laffer (Wanniski 1978)), expected tax revenues did not materialize, but rather continued to decline, and the budget failed to balance.

Not to be outdone, President Roosevelt hiked the top rate of the personal income tax to 79 per cent in 1936. In 1940, Roosevelt hiked the top rate of the income tax once again to a punitive 90 per cent (Reed 1981/2008). In 1941, Congress blocked his attempt to elevate it to 99.5 per cent on all incomes in excess of $100,000, a move more worthy of Roosevelt's contemporary, the Soviet dictator Joseph Stalin (or "Uncle Joe," as Roosevelt later fondly called him) than of the leader of a capitalist democracy. Following the refusal by Congress to enact this increase, Roosevelt attempted to issue an executive order to tax all income over $25,000 at 100 per cent: an order that was rescinded by an increasingly skeptical US Congress (Reed 1981/2008).

The 1937-38 economic contraction in particular, and indeed the whole decade of the 1930s, shows that punishing the successful is a disastrous way to promote economic recovery. People with high levels of wealth or entrepreneurial ability lose the incentive to invest and engage in business if they are not allowed to retain a significant proportion of the fruits of their efforts. Worse still, if up-front costs and risks are incurred in investing in physical or human capital,

---

[3]Andrew Mellon, the wealthy former Secretary of the Treasury and Samuel Insull, who had made a fortune supplying electricity to Chicago, were the two most famous targets of Roosevelt's attack dogs. Income tax charges were filed against both men, not because they had committed any clear violation of the IRS code, but because the prosecutions served to inflame public opinion against those "economic royalists", as Roosevelt typically characterized the wealthy.

highly taxed individuals must bear the costs and downside risk, but will not benefit from the upside. High marginal tax rates are a compelling explanation of the lethargy of business and investment throughout that decade.

After tax hikes, perhaps the worst policy intervention during the great economic contraction was the *Tariff Act* of 1930, signed into law by President Hoover. This protectionist legislation destroyed millions of jobs worldwide as other countries retaliated, leading to a dramatic reduction in the volume of international trade (Rowley, Thorbecke and Wagner 1995). It also played a major role in promoting the kind of economic nationalism that culminated in Mussolini's fascist state in Italy and in Hitler's Third Reich in Germany.

Within a month of the Great Crash, President Hoover convened conferences of business leaders urging them to keep wages artificially high, even as prices and profits were falling. While Hoover was a committed constitutionalist, and his policies were less invasive than those of his successor, this marked the beginning of government micromanagement of the economy. Ultimately policies such as these would result in significant increases in real wages as the economic contraction proceeded, hardly a policy designed to increase the level of employment.

This policy was pursued relentlessly by President Roosevelt, not least through the *National Industrial Recovery Act* of 1933. Cole and Ohanian (2004) attribute the persistence of the Depression largely to this Act. This legislation was designed to raise prices and wages and to establish planning boards charged with setting output goals for specific sectors of the economy. Undoubtedly, this ill-conceived, anti-market legislation intensified the economic contraction until the United States Supreme Court struck it down as unconstitutional in 1935 (Couch and Shughart 1998, Shughart 2004).

The *Agricultural Adjustment* Act of 1933, a similarly perverse intervention designed to reduce output and increase prices in the farming sector, also was struck down by the Supreme Court in 1936. In 1935, the *Wagner Act* encouraged union organization and legalized the closed shop, requiring union membership as a condition of employment. By cartelizing the labor market, this intervention escalated unemployment levels, especially within the industrial sectors of the economy (Couch and Shughart 1998, Shughart 2004).

2.5. FDR's assault on the Constitution and the rule of law

Herbert Hoover was a constitutionalist who respected the United States Constitution, the doctrine of *stare decisis*, legal precedent, and the rule of law. FDR was not. Roosevelt held no fixed political vision. Rather he was a pragmatist with a commitment to using the federal government to accomplish any tasks that he and his advisors thought necessary to move America forward, be it out of the Great Depression, or to victory over the Axis powers in the Second World War.

During the first one hundred days of Roosevelt's first administration, he signed into law legislation including the *Agricultural Adjustment Act* of 1933 (AAA) and the *National Industrial Recovery Act* of 1933 (NIRA) that created a number of federal regulatory agencies. A conservative bloc of Supreme Court Justices, referred to as the Four Horsemen (from *Revelation* 6: 2-8), in association with a changing mix of other Justices, struck powerful blows at the New Deal program on the ground that it interfered with the primacy of contract law over government regulation, as enforced consistently by the Supreme Court since the decisive judgment in *Lochner v. New York* (1905).

The Court voided the NIRA in *Schechter Poultry Corp. v. United States* (1935) and the AAA in *Carter v. Carter Coal* (1936). The Court also struck down a number of state regulatory laws (for example in *Morehead v. New York* (1936). Evidently, the Court was systematically shredding the New Deal on the ground that it violated the rule of law, as enshrined by precedent in prior Supreme Court constitutional interpretations.

Armed with a landslide re-election victory in 1936, a result that brought overwhelming Democratic majorities to the House of Representatives and to the Senate, FDR turned venomously not only on the Supreme Court, but also on the broader federal judiciary. He proposed a bill that would permit him to name additional justices to the Court and judges to the lower federal courts equal in number to jurists with ten years' of service who had attained the age of seventy and refused to retire.

This move provoked a shocked Congress into a majority opposition, and eventually the bill was allowed to die in the Senate Judiciary Committee. Nevertheless, the ruse succeeded. The Supreme Court blinked in *West Coast Hotel v. Parrish* (1937) by handing down by a 5-to-4 margin a decision upholding a state minimum wage law for women and minors, thus signaling a reversal of its hostility to state and federal legislation designed to regulate the economy. Justice Owen Roberts changed his allegiance to make this possible in "the switch in time that saved nine".

Roosevelt's assault on the United States Constitution was successful as each of the Four Horsemen sequentially retired and were replaced by New Deal activists. At the time of his death, the only seat on the Court not filled by FDR was that of Owen Roberts who had switched his vote under duress in 1937. And the Supreme Court's enforced supremacy of contract law over government regulation had dissipated.

2.6. Pessimistic expectations: a case of self-fulfilling prophecy?

A final cause of the depth of the depression was the negative feedback effects of the pessimistic expectations that kicked in during 1931, following the bank panic crisis and Britain's departure from the Gold Exchange Standard (Romer, C. 1990). From 1931, certainly until 1933, expectations throughout US society turned pessimistic, with households and firms believing that the deflation would intensify. In such an environment, households postponed consumption, to the extent that they were able, and businesses postponed investment plans. These reactions confirmed the validity of pessimistic expectations, as the US economy fell yet further into deflation.

However, pessimistic expectations are only in part an independent factor in the depression. They were in part a direct consequence of a sequence of ill-thought-out interventions and anti-capitalist threats by the Hoover, and especially, the Roosevelt administrations. While Roosevelt is known for the hopeful declaration that "the only thing we have to fear is fear itself," his rhetoric and his actions were far less encouraging to investors and businessmen. The pessimistic business expectations fueled by these and later anti-market enactments by Roosevelt and the Democratic Congress, especially following the 1937 unconstitutional capitulation of the Supreme Court, slowed down economic recovery and contributed to the second contraction in 1937-38. In consequence, the United States economy stagnated with high unemployment until the Second World War intervened in December 1941.

In conclusion, the Roosevelt administration pursued expansive monetary and fiscal policies that would later be viewed as Keynesian, throughout the period 1933 to 1939. These policies were accompanied by a few years of tepid recovery, without ever raising the economy back to its 1929 level; but they dramatically failed to restore the United States economy to full employment. The explanation for this failure is not to be found in a "liquidity trap" (which did not exist), nor in a failure of "animal spirits" to lift private investment outlays sufficiently. They failed because consumption multipliers were far lower than Keynes suggested, because FDR's fiscal stimulus expenditures were targeted cynically to swing votes in the Electoral College rather than to areas of relatively high unemployment (Couch and Shughart 1998, Couch and Shughart 2000, Higgs 1987, Shughart 2004), and because dramatic increases in tax rates and widespread anti-business interventions embalmed the United States economy in pessimistic expectations and created a climate of fear of profit-expropriations that suppressed private investment.

2.7. CONCLUSION: A FAILURE OF GOVERNMENT

In 1936, J. M. Keynes' General Theory introduced a new theoretical framework that accounted for the depression in terms of a "paradox of thrift" a "liquidity trap", and the failing "animal spirits" of investors, denied that the market possessed equilibrating mechanisms, and called full-employment equilibrium a "special case," which rarely obtains in reality. All this was much too clever.

A single highly unusual historical episode is not a sound basis for a "general theory," and before and after the Great Depression the US economy has, most of the time, fairly closely approximated a situation in which those who are willing to work for the going wage can find jobs. Traditional Keynesian theory has quietly fallen out of fashion among economists for a generation, for reasons that are gently expressed in the following disclaimer in a leading graduate macro textbook:

> Traditional Keynesian models ... often directly specify relationships among aggregate variables. The relationships are often static, and the models' implications for the behavior of some variables (such as the capital stock) are often omitted from the analysis. In addition, rather than specifying stochastic processes for the exogenous variables, the analysis focuses on the effect of one-time changes. And the models are so stylized that any effort to see how well they match overall features of the economy is of little value. (Romer, D. 2006, 222)

David Romer (2006) might be reluctant to put it this way, but what we glean from this passage (and from the track record of Keynesianism generally) is that Keynesian theory has been exposed as theoretically flawed and empirically invalid. Even before the rational expectations revolution, the permanent income hypothesis (Friedman 1957) suggested that fiscal multipliers were minimal in the case of income injections viewed as transient rather than permanent, while Robert Mundell and Michael Fleming separately demonstrated that any fiscal stimulus impacts the exchange rate rather than the real economy in the case of open economies operating under floating exchange rates (Mundell 1968, Fleming 1962).

The rational expectations literature has further weakened the argument for Keynesian fiscal stimulus by demonstrating that anticipated fiscal expansion will be largely neutralized by private actors within an economy (Lucas 1975, 1976). The widespread "stagflation" of the 1970s evidenced that the Phillips Curve was upward-sloping rather then downward-sloping in price inflation/level of unemployment space, completely counter to the Keynesian predictions of Samuelson and Solow (1960). Yet, discredited hydraulic Keynesian economics is once again fashionable among United States economists, especially among the top economic advisors appointed by President Obama (See Romer, C.D.,1990, 1992, 1993, Summers 1988).

What lessons do the experiences of the 1930s hold for policymakers today? The American national myth that FDR and the New Deal "pulled the US out of the Great Depression" does not stand up to an examination of the facts.

FDR's money and banking policies were an improvement over those of Herbert Hoover, and probably aided the partial recovery of 1933-37. Overall, however, FDR and the New Deal prolonged the Great Depression (Powell 2003). Especially destructive were tax hikes, trade protectionism, the micro policies of the NIRA, and a rise in union privilege. Throughout the Great Depression, inefficient public choice pressures dominated market-efficiency considerations in fueling the policy responses of Herbert Hoover and FDR to the economic exigencies of their times (Couch and Shughart 1998, Shughart 2004).

Writing in 1936, Keynes advocated expansionary fiscal policy to get the economy moving. By this time, the Hoover and Roosevelt administrations had already been engaged in deficit spending for several years. While there is a certain short-run correlation between deficit spending and growth during the 1929-1945 period, which provides some substantiation for Keynes's view, the monetarist explanation championed by Milton Friedman and others (Friedman and Schwartz 1963) is much better able to explain why the Depression occurred in the first place, as well as why the limited 1933-37 recovery occurred.

In any case, the peacetime recovery was unusually brief and left the economy below its 1929 level, the first time that a business cycle had peaked lower than its predecessor. Keynesian fiscal policy did not "stimulate" the economy, but burdened it, leaving unemployment high and growth well below trend. The unemployment problem was resolved only by forcibly drafting large numbers of individuals into the US military at the onset of the Second World War. The shortfall in aggregate demand was resolved only by the massive build-up of materiel for the European and the Pacific theaters as the United States was dragged unwillingly into armed combat by the Japanese sneak attack on Pearl Harbor in December 1941.

Surely, as Posner (2009) suggests, serious mistakes made within the capitalist system played an important role in bringing about the financial crisis of 1929. Householders had assumed unsustainable amounts of mortgage debt, without any prodding from favorable tax laws or government pro-home-ownership propaganda. Households had borrowed from banks to purchase stocks on margin, leveraging their debt unsustainably during a stock market bubble. Banks had participated equally in such risky activities, without any encouragement from government-provided deposit insurance.

Ultimately, however, these capitalist failures were driven by the loose money policies of a government agency, the Federal Reserve, throughout the "Roaring '20s", under the mismanagement of Benjamin Strong, encouraged by his Bank of England counterpart, Montague Norman. Once the financial crisis occurred, the irresponsible behavior of the Hoover and the Roosevelt administrations, compounded by the disastrous behavior of the Federal Reserve ensured that a minor recession collapsed into a decade-long economic depression. Most damaging of all, from the longer-term perspective, was FDR's behavior in compromising the US Constitution, weakening its protection of individual liberty and free-enterprise capitalism (Rowley 2005).

Posner (2009) simply fails to apply his usual well-balanced pragmatism to the reality of this economic episode. The economic failure was that of government, not of capitalism.

3

George W. Keynes and Franklin Delano Obama: The 2007-9 Financial and Economic Collapse: Causes and Consequences

K eynesian economics (and we do mean old-style Keynesianism, not New Keynesian Rational Expectations) has suddenly and surprisingly become fashionable once again among many US economists, especially those working within the Obama administration. Hydraulic Keynesianism, and fiscal policy as a tool of macroeconomic management in particular, had been in retreat for more than a quarter of a century; yet the crisis seems to have convinced many economists (some, like Richard Posner, formerly in the free market camp) that any alternative to the allegedly conservative economics applied by the Bush administration deserves more than another look.

The irony is that the outdated economics applied by the Bush administration was not "conservative", except for the initial tax cuts that he signed into law at the beginning of his first term in office. All his later economic policies turned out to be hydraulic Keynesian. The expansionary monetary and especially fiscal policies, that Keynesian economists (like Joseph Stiglitz, Paul Krugman, Bradford De Long, Laurence Summers and Christina Romer) are now vigorously promoting, were implemented during the 2001-2002 recession, and the years that followed, by the Bush administration and a compliant Congress, supported by the Federal Reserve Board under Chairman Alan Greenspan and Governor (and from 2006, Chairman) Ben Bernanke.

What old-fashioned Keynesian economists are now advocating and what the left-leaning Obama administration is actually implementing, is a much larger dose of what took us to where we are.

"Give me that old-time religion.
Give me that old-time religion.
It was good enough for W.
It is more than good enough for me."

3.1. THE GREAT 1990S BOOM AND ITS AFTERMATH

The great New Economy boom of the 1990s has acquired a reputation as illusory, transient, a "bubble." This judgment reflects the stock market decline after 2000, when the Dow fell almost 40 per cent, and the NASDAQ over 70 per cent, erasing trillions of dollars of paper wealth. Yet, even those who invested in the stock market did not do badly from the New Economy. A person who invested in a Dow index fund in January 1995 (DJIA: 3,834) would have earned annual returns of over 25 per cent over a five-year period by the time the Dow reached its peak in January 2000 (DJIA: 11,901). A person who invested in a NASDAQ index fund would have seen his wealth grow 600 per cent by March 2000! Some of these gains were then lost, but even an investor who sold at the low points of these indices in 2001 and 2002 would have nearly doubled his money, not a bad rate of return over six or seven years.

In February 2000, as the Dow began a long slide, *The Economist* paid tribute to the boom in an article entitled "America's amazing expansion: in due course it will stop. Until then, one stands in awe."

> Another month, another record. America's expansion has just entered its 107th month, making it the longest on record. Such longevity is impressive-though not unheard of (East Asia grew for decades before its crash and Japan's economy roared for 15 years before its bubble burst in the early 1990s). Even more impressive is the nature of America's boom.
>
> This expansion bears scant resemblance to its post-war predecessors, and it has flouted several economic laws. Traditionally in America, an unemployment rate of less than 5.5% has triggered inflationary pressures. The jobless rate has been below 5% since July 1997; yet, until recently, wage and price pressures have been conspicuously absent. Traditionally, productivity growth has slowed as expansions have matured, with firms obliged to draw less-skilled workers from the depleted pool of labour. But in this boom, productivity growth has actually risen as the recovery has gone on.
>
> This has been, in short, a most unusual expansion. (*The Economist*, 2/3/2000)

The sense of "awe" that many shared with *The Economist* in 2000 has dulled with time. It deserves to be renewed. After all, none of what was written in the quote needs to be revised in hindsight. On the contrary, the New Economy was real, and not even entirely transient. Unemployment, though it has never returned to its 2000 low of 4 per cent, remained in a low 4.5 per cent to 6 per cent range throughout most of George W. Bush's two terms in office. The productivity acceleration of the late 1990s actually *accelerated further* after 2000: annual productivity growth in 2001-2004 was 3.1 per cent, compared to 2.6 per cent in 1997-2000. The 1990s, the last decade of the twenty year period of the Great Moderation, remain the best practical paradigm of sustained prosperity there is.

The 2001 recession proved that the 'Goldilocks' economy had not killed the business cycle; but it was the mildest recession in decades. At the time, however, there were fears of another Great Depression. *The Economist*, so often a barometer of the state of elite opinion, had worried in a 1999 survey of the world economy that:

> Indeed, there are remarkable similarities with America in the 1920s and Japan in the 1980s … In the 1920s, people also believed in a new era of faster growth arising from new technology. The only difference was that at that time most of the excitement was generated by cars, aeroplanes, electrification and the radio, rather than by computers, telecoms and the Internet. (9/23/1999)

The Economist's main fear was of a bubble in asset prices, at that time mainly stocks, but also housing prices, which became more of a problem later. Low unemployment, low inflation, and high productivity growth were also features, seemingly benign, that the New Economy of the 1990s shared with America's "Roaring Twenties" and with 1980s Japan. Since the "Roaring Twenties" were followed by the Great Depression, and Japan's 1980s boom by the "lost decade" of the 1990s, there was good reason to worry.

After the stock market (collapsing dot-coms-driven) declines of 2000, the top concern of economic policymakers was to prevent this grim scenario from recurring. This became especially urgent after the 9/11 terrorist attacks in 2001. The symbolic resonance of the site of the most successful attack, the World Trade Center, made it clear that the terrorists were targeting America's economy and way of life, and a major economic disruption might well have been perceived as a success for the terrorists and thus undermined America's national will. To prevent a feared economic collapse, the Bush administration, Congress, and Alan Greenspan's Federal Reserve adopted the most expansionary fiscal and monetary policy stance America had experienced since the 1970s.

3.2. FISCAL AND MONETARY POLICY IN THE BUSH ERA WERE HIGHLY EXPANSIONARY (KEYNESIAN)

In the 1980s, the fiscal policy of the Reagan administration was highly expansionary, while the monetary policy of Paul Volcker's Federal Reserve was strongly restrictive, as the Federal Reserve struggled to put out-of-control inflation back in its cage. After 1995, Federal Reserve policy was more expansionary, as the M2 money supply expanded and asset prices, though not consumer prices, rose sharply. But fiscal policy was not expansionary: the large budget deficits of the Reagan era subsided and were replaced by budget surpluses in Clinton's second term of office.

So, in the two decades before 2001, fiscal and monetary policies tended to offset each other, and were never both expansionary at the same time. After 2001, in an attempt at Keynesian stimulus, fiscal policy returned to deficit spending, while the Federal Reserve lowered interest rates and expanded M2 still further. Both the fiscal and monetary furnaces now blazed at the same time.

Figure 2 depicts the historical time-path of real federal debt per capita in the United States from the outset of war in 1941 until the onset of economic contraction in 2007-08.

Following a flood of federal debt to finance the Second World War, real federal debt per capita in the United States declined gradually as a result of approximate budget balance through the relatively conservative 1950s, and as a result of monetizing rising budget deficits via inflation throughout the 1960s and 1970s. After 1980, aggressive disinflation by Paul Volcker's Federal Reserve put an end to monetization of the debt.

However, budget deficits spiked dramatically as the Reagan administration pursued Keynesian fiscal policies involving a defense build-up and an ongoing rise in social expenditures. Real federal debt per capita almost doubled during Reagan's two terms, the fastest rate of growth in the history of the Republic apart from the Second World War. This rise persisted throughout the administration of George Herbert Walker Bush and into the administration of Bill Clinton.

The deficit was gradually brought under control by tax hikes and spending restraint, by the "peace dividend" after the end of the Cold War, and by the early fiscal discipline imposed by the 1994 Republican-led Congress. During the

Figure 2: Real federal debt per capita, 1940-2007 (2007$)

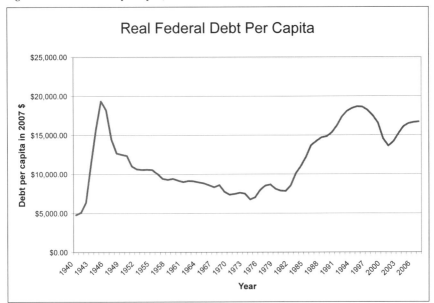

Source: Authors' calculations based on data from Office of Management and Budget, US Census Bureau, Bureau of Labor Statistics

final years of the fiscally conservative Clinton administration, the federal budget actually moved into surplus (ignoring unfunded commitments) and the real value of the US per capita federal debt began to decline.

While George W. Bush's administration increased the size of the real per capita debt, it can be seen in Figure 2 that deficits increased less under the younger President Bush than they had during the Reagan administration. These deficits were partly an "automatic" result of the recession, and partly a side-effect of the War on Terror after 9/11, but they also resulted from significant fiscal policy shifts, reflecting a Keynesian effort to stimulate the economy.

In February 2009, the total US federal debt was $12.35 trillion. Of this, approximately $6.45 trillion was held by the public and $5.9 trillion in the form of intra-governmental holdings. The per capita burden of the debt roughly tripled in real terms between 1980 and 2008. These figures increase dramatically if the present values of all unfunded federal entitlement programs are taken into account.

Figure 3 explains in more detail how the real federal debt per capita grew over the period 1929 to 2008. Our discussion focuses on experience over the period 2001-2008, referenced against the period 1960 to 2000. After rising steeply from 1960 to 1975 – real federal spending per capita almost doubled in this period, increasing from $4,764 per capita to $9,069 – spending growth slowed during the later 1970s and 1980s and then, from 1992 it came to a standstill, stabilizing at about $12,500 per capita for a decade.

This respite from growth of the burden of government was a bipartisan achievement and is probably the biggest single explanation of that extraordinary prosperity of the "New Economy" of the Clinton years, discussed above. Unfortunately, federal spending growth was only asleep, not dead. After 2001, it woke up. Real federal expenditure per capita started rising again, at an annual growth rate of 2.45 per cent. This was still well below the 4.31 per cent averaged over the period 1960 to 1975.

While the Bush tax cuts have sometimes been blamed for the rising deficits, it was not a reduction in tax revenues that caused the debt to grow. Tax revenues and social insurance contributions in 2007, at $13,866 per capita, were

Figure 3: A growing burden of government, with a brief respite in the 1990s

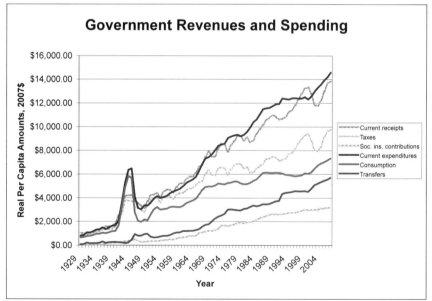

Source: BEA Table 3.1, US Census Bureau, BLS (CPI)

higher than their 2000 levels. Rather, deficits appeared because of the collapse of spending discipline. President Bush in particular was notoriously reluctant to use the presidential veto to contain pork-barrel spending by a spendthrift Republican-dominated Congress, and he also signed into law a new entitlement program, the Medicare prescription drug benefit, as well as legislation increasing energy and defense spending.

Fiscal policy became expansionary after 2000. Monetary policy had already been expansionary and became more so. **Figure 4** traces movements in real monetary aggregates per capita in the United States over the period 1960 to 2008.

The three monetary aggregates shown are (a) currency, (b) M1 and (c) M2. In terms of 2007 dollars, currency per capita remains within the range $1,000-$1,300 between 1960 and 1985. It then increases at a steady rate, reaching $2,670 in 2008. This latter figure is well in excess of the amount held by typical U.S. households for transaction and precautionary reasons, and reflects the increasingly widespread use of the U.S. dollar as a vehicular currency throughout the world. M1 is quite stable throughout the entire period, but changes in the nature of the financial system (online banking, debit cards) render this monetary aggregate misleading.

Figure 4: Monetary aggregates, 1960-2008

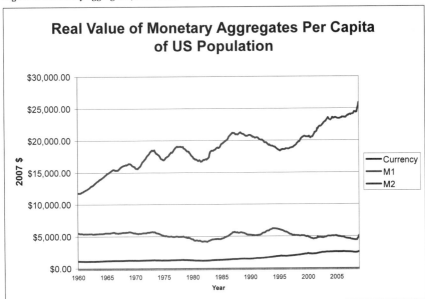

Source: Federal Reserve, US Census Bureau, BLS

M2, the broader monetary aggregate, is the most relevant indicator of the effective monetary environment. M2 per capita rose smoothly and sharply in the 1960s, became more volatile in the 1970s, sharply declined sharply during the early 1980s under the anti-inflationary policy of Federal Reserve Chairman, Paul Volcker, resumed its volatility, and reached a peak of $21,229 per capita in 1988. M2 then steadily declined to a low of $18,379 per capita in 1995. Then, between 1996 and 2008, the M2 money supply increased steadily reaching $25,902 per capita by the end of 2008.

M2 growth reflects a monetary policy by Federal Reserve Chairman Alan Greenspan, and to a lesser extent by Chairman Ben Bernanke, which in hindsight can be characterized as expansionary, especially after 2000, as Greenspan sought to counter perceived recessionary impacts of the collapse of the dot.com bubble and the 9/11 terrorist attacks, and kept interest rates low in 2003 and 2004, when recovery was well underway.

Under Chairman Greenspan, the M2 monetary aggregate growth rate exceeded 8 per cent per annum throughout the period 2001-2003. This expansion was accompanied by the lowering of the Fed Fund Rate from 6.25 per cent in early 2001 to 1.75 per cent by the end of the year. The Federal Reserve continued to lower the rate further throughout 2002 and 2003, holding it at 1 per cent until mid-2004. The real Federal Funds Rate was negative for an unprecedented two and a half years (White 2009).

Essentially, over the period 2001-2006, the Federal Reserve ignored the Taylor Rule (Taylor 2009) in deploying its monetary policy. The Taylor Rule says that the interest rate should be one-and-a-half times the inflation rate plus one-half times the GDP gap (that measures how far GDP is over its normal trend level) plus one. If this Rule had been followed, interest rates would have risen from 2 percent to 5 percent over the period 2001-2005 instead of trailing around one percent until mid-2004. The stock market and house price bubbles would have been checked off well before the financial collapse occurred.

By lowering short-term interest rates relative to 30-year rates that were much less responsive to monetary policy, Greenspan opened up incentives for cash-strapped house-buyers to resort to adjustable rate mortgages (ARMS) typically based on one-year interest rates. The share of new mortgages with adjustable rates, only one-fifth in 2001, had more than doubled by 2004. The resetting of these, at higher rates for high-risk customers, in 2008-9 has proved to be a significant source of house foreclosures in the United States.

Tax cuts and deficit spending, M2 money supply growth, and low interest rates, made the period 2001 through 2007 the most expansionary economic policy environment in the United States since the 1970s. The Bush administration, the GOP-majority Congress, and the Greenspan Federal Reserve were, in effect if not in name, engaged in a great Keynesian experiment. And in the short run, it appeared to succeed.

The recession of 2001-2002 turned out to be one of the shallowest in decades. US GDP growth quickly resumed, unemployment rose only mildly and soon began to come down again. And the *world* economy began booming too: the years 2004-2007 were the best years for developing countries since the 1970s. Growth in developing countries in these years approached 8 per cent, almost double the rates that prevailed in the 1980s and 1990s. But it appears now that this worldwide boom depended on unsustainable current-account imbalances and increases in personal indebtedness in many of the developed countries.

Thanks to economic theory, and the experience of the 1970s, economic technocrats in the US executive branch and in the Congressional Budget Office are well aware that an excessively expansionary policy stance has its dangers. So why did the federal government respond so acquiescently to the economic excesses that culminated in the present crash?

In the case of elected politicians, the problem is structural: democracy appears to have a perennial or permanent bias towards deficit spending, which may be contained only by some fundamental change in constitutional rules (Buchanan and Wagner 1978, Buchanan, Rowley and Tollison 1986). One such rule change, which has been widely adopted internationally in recent decades, is an independent central bank. But, in this case, the US Federal Reserve, although not beholden to electoral interests, also adopted a dangerously permissive stance. The reason is that measured inflation remained low. Why? Why did the fiscal and monetary furnaces of the Bush years not apparently fuel a surge in stagflation, such as occurred dramatically in the 1970s?

3.3. CONSUMER PRICE INFLATION REMAINED SUBDUED DUE TO RISING PRODUCTIVITY, GLOBALIZATION, AND CAPITAL INFLOWS

The short answer is that they did. Excessive money growth since 1995 caused first, stock market price inflation, and then house price inflation. What did not occur is *consumer* price inflation.

Four factors combined to divert inflationary pressures into asset prices and keep consumer prices stable. First, globalization created favorable terms-of-trade effects (for *both* sides of the rich-poor divide), as US consumers gained access to low-priced imports from developing countries with low labor costs, especially

China (and as US demand fueled high growth in Asia and elsewhere). Second, rising productivity caused "technological deflation" which offset inflationary pressures resulting from money growth.

Third, for whatever reason, perhaps in hopes of insuring themselves against a rerun of the financial and currency crises of 1997-99, the rest of the world gained a huge appetite for US federal government liabilities, and willingly financed large and growing US trade deficits. Finally, household expenditures were diverted first into stocks and business investment, then, disastrously, into the housing market (Bernanke 2009).

House and stock prices are not included in the Consumer Price Index (CPI) which is used to construct the inflation statistics that provide a basis for policy (Greenlees and McClelland 2008). The value of a house, in particular, has been excluded from the CPI since 1983. Instead, the index includes a measure called rental equivalence. During the house price bubble, the rental equivalence measure understated the true impact of house price inflation on the CPI, and thus enabled the Federal Reserve to continue a more expansionary monetary policy than was justified from the viewpoint of holding price inflation to an annual rate of 2 to 3 per cent.

The fact that house price growth outpaced rental rates suggests that owning and renting are not perfect substitutes, in which case the substitution of rental equivalence for house value might be inappropriate as a measure of consumer prices. The use of rental equivalence instead of house value had a large effect on measured inflation, significantly under-stating it over the period 2001 to mid-year 2006, and significantly over-stating it thereafter. This serious error of measurement has had a damaging impact on monetary policy.

Figure 5 tracks the behavior of the *Consumer Price Index* (CPI) and the *House Price Index* (HPI) over the period 1976 to 2008. Consumer prices have been fairly stable since the early 1980s. Following the shift in Federal Reserve Policy in favor of a monetarist policy of containing price inflation, pulling down the rate of price inflation from 15 per cent in 1979 to 3 per cent in 1984, the CPI has fluctuated within a relatively narrow and much lower range over the past quarter of a century. Since 2000, despite an expansionist monetary policy, the CPI has fluctuated between 1.8 per cent and 4 per cent per annum.

House prices have been much more volatile. This divergence became especially marked after 2000, with house price inflation rising to over 10 per cent in 2005 and 2006. If the Federal Reserve had considered it a priority to keep house prices stable, monetary policy would have been tighter for several years after 2001, and would have been looser from the third quarter of 2006 onwards.

Such a monetary policy might well have completely averted the financial crisis of September 2008.

Figure 5: The "Great Moderation" looks quite inflationary if housing prices are taken into account

Source: Office of Federal Housing Enterprise Oversight, BLS

3.4. EASY MONEY FUELED A HOUSE PRICE BUBBLE, LOW INTEREST RATES, AND A SURGE IN PERSONAL INDEBTEDNESS

Instead of causing CPI inflation, M2 money growth in the period 1995-2007, and especially after 2001, had the effect of driving down real rates of interest. **Figure 6** puts this in a historical context by outlining the movement of real interest rates over the period 1955 to 2008.

The Volcker disinflation is dramatically visible in **Figure 6**, with real interest rates spiking from negative levels in the late 1970s to 8-10 per cent in the case of corporate bonds in 1983-84. While real interest rates on Treasuries and Certificates of Deposit were somewhat erratic, AAA corporate bonds paid between 4 per cent and 6 per cent throughout the years 1987-2002. After 2002, however, all real interest rates fell sharply. Since 2007, the real interest rate on short-term CDs and Treasuries has been negative, even though the rate of price inflation remains low.

Figure 6: Nominal interest rates fell to unsustainably low levels in the 2000s

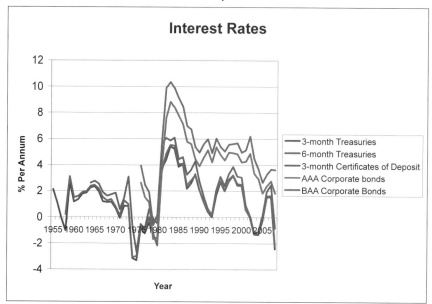

An interest rate is a price. In particular, it is the price of debt. When the price of something falls, the quantity demanded rises. So it is not surprising that these low interest rates led to a widespread surge in indebtedness throughout the US economy. While the rise in debt looks like a time bomb from the vantage point of 2009, debt is not necessarily a bad thing. It can be a reasonable way for individuals to smooth consumption over the life-cycle.

Figure 7 tracks the behavior of household debt over the period 1975 to 2008, separating out consumer and mortgage debt and then aggregating the two sources. As is evident from Figure 7, consumer debt has been rising linearly and mortgage debt has been rising exponentially throughout this period (Hodges 2009, Hoover Institution 2009)).

The rise in consumer debt shown in Figure 7 reflects the response of consumers to low interest rates. In October 2008, consumer debt stood at $2.58 trillion, amounting to a per capita debt of $8,500. Approximately 37 per cent of consumer debt took the form of revolving credit, defined as credit that is repeatedly available as periodic payments are made. The most common form of revolving credit is credit card debt. The remaining 63 per cent took the form of non-revolving debt, most notably involving automobile loans. In 2008, the av-

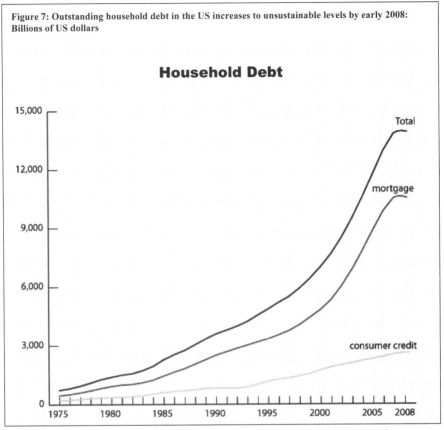

Figure 7: Outstanding household debt in the US increases to unsustainable levels by early 2008: Billions of US dollars

erage down-payment on a new car was only 7 per cent of the car's purchase price. As credit terms tightened, following the financial crisis of September 2008, the leveraged impact on household consumption was very sharp.

The rise in home mortgage debt reflects both a response to low interest rates and a house price bubble. Home mortgage debt at that time stood at $11.2 trillion (approximately 80 per cent of total household debt), or $42,400 per capita. Per capita debt thus amounted to over $50,000, well above the median household income in the United States. The distribution of this debt was highly skewed. Approximately 23 per cent of households had no debt at all, and approximately 54 per cent of all households had no consumer debt.

The trigger for the liquidity crisis was an increase in sub-prime mortgage defaults in February 2007 (Brunnermeier 2009). Much of the home buying and home refinancing that took place in 2001-2007, even by ordinary people, seems to have had a speculative character, as home buyers either hoped to gain from permanently as prices rose still further. Some households that entered the mortgage market never remotely had the wherewithal to finance their mortgages (Bernanke 2009).

In many cases, lenders or borrowers or both seem to have been fully aware of this situation, and a large number of unscrupulous realtors encouraged their clients to write "liars' contracts" in which borrowers were encouraged to overstate their income and net wealth to qualify for higher mortgages. To enable buyers to access the market, lenders provided mortgages in excess of the market value of the houses, and buyers entered into mortgage commitments that put them underwater right at the outset of the transaction.

Two major private but government-sponsored enterprises that securitized some fifty percent of all U.S. mortgages, *The Federal National Mortgage Association* (Fannie Mae), and *The Federal Home Loan Mortgage Corporation* (Freddie Mac), were also complicit, indeed, were active players in this subterfuge. Operating under all-but non-existent oversight by their completely captive regulator, *The Federal Housing Finance Agency*, these companies aggressively (and allegedly in some instances, fraudulently) pursued government policies designed, for vote-seeking purposes, to extend home ownership as broadly as possible.

Politicians treated the home ownership rate as a political-economic variable to be maximized. Thus, Bush told the Republican National Convention in 2004: "Thanks to our policies, home ownership in America is at an all-time high. Tonight we set a new goal: seven million more affordable homes in the next 10 years so more American families will be able to open the door and say 'Welcome to my home'" (Bush 2004).

Presidents and legislators of both parties promoted the growth of this masked subsidy of home ownership for two decades before *Fannie Mae* and *Freddie Mac* went bust in September 2008 when the long-implicit taxpayer guarantee was made explicit. *Fannie Mae* and *Freddie Mac* would never have existed in a free housing market and should surely have been liquidated in September 2008.

Ideally, the cautionary tale they provide should serve to remind informed voters and, thus, their elected representatives, not to create "government-sponsored enterprises" in the future. Realistically, of course, this will not happen. Memories quickly fade as politicians sense new minority vote opportunities through manipulating the mortgage market to allow access to financially unqualified would-be customers. A government-induced house-price bubble is as natural a phenomenon as a Bernard Madoff Ponzi-scheme in an environment of over-easy money. Indeed, the two operations are conducted by like-minded opportunistic individuals for very similar self-seeking purposes, personal wealth in the case of Madoff, personal votes in the case of politicians and presidents.

The three major credit-rating agencies, Fitch, Moody's and Standard and Poor, were also a major part of the problem. Driven by pursuit of short-term profit to flout conflict of interest guidelines, they continued rating toxic securities AAA, rather than condemning them to junk-bond status (Grynbaum 2008). This behavior went unchallenged by a *Securities Exchange Commission* that, by 2007, had largely abandoned its regulatory responsibilities and had assumed a "Stockholm Syndrome" role as eager captive to the very organizations that it was supposed to regulate (Stigler 1971, Peltzman 1976).

The excesses of the housing bubble thus reflected a mixture of private market failure and government failure. The pattern was that individuals, banks, and companies were "writing naked puts," taking bets whereby the upside would go to them, the downside, since it would leave them unable to fulfill their obligations, would fall to someone else, who ultimately is turning out to be the taxpayer, forced by government and its 'independent' agencies into bailing out large numbers of thoroughly undeserving organizations, individuals, and government agencies.

In effect, private lenders, private borrowers, elected politicians, and "government-sponsored enterprises" gambled that continuously rising house prices would cover rationally expected income shortfalls. Such behavior was not irrational. Rather, it reflected the perverse incentives that arise in situations of asset price inflation, which government and the Federal Reserve actively promoted, together with the expectation that taxpayers would rescue them from the adverse consequences of their misbehavior. Of course, those who bought houses and "flipped" them before the prices crashed made money, and their success lured others into the market.

3.5. The return of debt-deflation

While debt can be individually rational, in an excessively large aggregate, it makes the economy vulnerable in a deflation (*The Economist* February 14, 2009, 73-75). Loans are typically secured by some kind of real asset as collateral. As long as the collateral is worth more than the dollar amount of the loan, it is incentive-compatible for the borrower to repay the loan rather than lose his collateral. Deflation reduces the dollar value of collateral. Consumers who find that the collateral, for example, a house or an automobile, against which they secure a loan, is worth less than what they owe may find it in their interest to walk away, with or without declaring bankruptcy. Thus a serious monetary policy error creates a major institutional problem.

The financial turmoil began in the market for US sub-prime mortgages and the markets for structured products based on them (BIS 78th Annual Report, 2008, 4). Delinquency rates in the sub-prime market had started to rise in early 2005, even while house prices were rising. This was initially a side effect of the willingness of lenders to lower standards to increase the volume of business in a booming market. Later, as house prices began to decline, mortgage delinquencies accelerated, and began to encroach upon a larger class of borrowers. By this time, the financial industry had developed the practice of "securitizing" mortgages, a method of converting ordinary mortgages into complex financial instruments. Trillions of dollars' worth of mortgage-backed securities had swamped the financial system.

3.6. THE FINANCIAL COLLAPSE

In early 2007, credit spreads on mortgage-backed securities began to widen and rating downgrades increased. In August 2007, a small number of investment banks froze redemptions, citing an inability to value their assets. From this inconspicuous beginning, financial disruption spread through every corner of the financial system (BIS 2008, Bernanke 2009).

By early August 2007, concern about the valuations of complex products, liquidity risk, and counterparty risk negatively affected a large number of financial markets. The market for structured products based on mortgages collapsed, followed by a major withdrawal of investors from the asset-backed commercial paper market. Inter-bank term money markets in the major currencies simply froze, as evidenced by an unprecedented gap between policy interest rates (over a one-to-three month horizon) and the rates at which the largest banks were prepared to lend to each other. The speed at which this collapse occurred took almost everyone by surprise.

Financial services differ from other industries because so much of the business is writing bets (*The Economist*, January 24, 2009). One party pays the other for a claim that comes good, for example, if oil prices fall, or a company defaults on its bonds, or householders make their mortgage payments on time. For every loser on a credit-default swap, there is a corresponding winner. The claims net to zero.

However, the winners and the losers behave differently, so that the winners' extra spending may not offset the losers' retrenchment. And the losers may not be able to pay up either because they are insolvent, or because they are illiquid. This *counterparty risk*, which grows with the volume of bets, has been the outstanding feature of the current financial crisis.

For example, *American International Group* (AIG), once the world's biggest insurer, was bailed out in October 2008 by the US government when it became clear that it was unable to honor its vast one-way bets (credit-default swaps) on financial stability. Had AIG failed, the banks and other financial institutions on the other side of the bargain would have been in serious (though ultimately self-induced) trouble, because they had mistakenly put their trust in AIG, without properly factoring in the systemic risk of its default.

To make matters worse, many of the bets took the form of extremely complex asset bundles, bundles too complicated, it would seem, for those who held them to value in terms of mark-to-market rules. This implies that virtually every major bank in the United States may be underwater with respect to such bundled assets. Several such banks are technically insolvent under strict "mark-to-market" accounting rules. Worse still, several of the major U.S. banks threw caution to the winds as the housing market bubble fueled its way upwards, and invested in such assets to a degree that, in the wake of the stock market crash, far outstrips standard regulatory requirements.

Bank regulators measure the adequacy of bank reserves in several ways. The most prominent, but essentially flawed, measure, *Tier 1 capital*, requires banks to hold $6 in capital for every $100 in loans and other commitments. This money is intended to serve as a buffer against losses. However, financial analysts have long emphasized a preference for capital raised from the most basic sources, *tangible common equity* (TCE), which counts as capital only money raised from basic sources such as quarterly profits and the sale of common stock.

Most financial analysts regard $3-$4 in tangible common equity for $100 in assets as the absolute minimum acceptable ratio. By this standard, perhaps fifty per cent of the largest 19 U.S. banks fail the regulatory test at this time and several, including *Citigroup Bank* and the *Bank of America*, would already be in receivership in the absence of government cash injections (which incidentally count as part of the TCE ratio only if they comprise common stock).

In March 2008, the prestigious investment bank and bond trader, *Bear Stearns* was rescued from bankruptcy via a shotgun marriage with the healthiest major US bank, *JP Morgan Chase*, brokered by the Bush administration – a largely unnoticed harbinger of the coming financial storm. In mid-September 2008, the true depth of the financial crisis would become public knowledge. A second failing investment bank, *Lehman Brothers* was allowed to go into receivership, with *Barclay's Bank* successfully cherry-picking over its more valuable assets. The world's largest insurance company, *AIG*, which had ventured unwisely and extensively into financial markets, was bailed out by the Bush administration on the dubious ground that "it was too big to fail".

Also in September 2008, shotgun marriages of financially defaulting financial institutions such as *Merrill Lynch* (with *The Bank of America*) and *Wachovia* (with *Citigroup*) coerced by the Bush administration through threats of removing the institutions' CEOs and Boards of Directors if they failed to comply with its demands, further damaged the balance sheets of two already suspect giant banks. In April 2009, justifiably angry shareholders ousted Kenneth Lewis from his position as Chairman of the *Bank of America* (though he retained his position as Chief Executive Officer), for his perceived unwillingness to defend shareholder rights when acquiescing to government pressure to acquire *Merrill Lynch*, thereby rendering his bank insolvent.

As credit dried up, and major bank-runs were averted only by the existence of comprehensive FDIC deposit-protection, the real economy was severely impacted and the economic contraction that had started gently, late in 2007, became substantially more serious. In the final stages of a divisive 2008 Presidential Election campaign, the US electorate unexpectedly became aware that the economy was in recession.

In effect, by 2007, speculation on rising house prices had penetrated a huge part of the economy. To an extent that is clear only in retrospect, much of the financial industry, a substantial share of the US population, the Bush administration, and the US Congress had all placed bets greater than their collective net worth (economic or political) on house prices continuing to rise. Many companies and individuals lost heavily on their bad bets, but the trouble is that when they could not absorb the losses, these losses fell on counter-parties or on the taxpayer.

To the extent that this was anticipated *ex ante*, business decisions that were disastrous from a commercial point of view may have been rational for the private individuals and firms that made them. It is a case of "heads I win, tails, the taxpayer loses." Since the median American voter is a homeowner, government intervention in the event of a house price collapse was always likely. By this analysis, behind the crisis lay a peculiar form of moral hazard.

3.7. PUBLIC DEBT AND BUSINESS INVESTMENT: A VIRGINIA POLITICAL ECONOMY PERSPECTIVE

We have seen that expansionary monetary policy played a role in causing the crisis. What about fiscal policy? Did the Bush administration's Keynesian-style deficit spending precipitate the crisis?

Economists of the Virginia school have long argued that democracy has an inbuilt bias towards deficit spending (Buchanan and Wagner 1978, Buchanan,

Rowley and Tollison 1986, Rowley, Shughart and Tollison 2002). For a brief period in the late 1990s, these arguments seemed to be obsolete. Deficits had been brought under control and then turned into surpluses (excluding unfunded liabilities). Under the presidency of George W. Bush, as we have seen, deficits made a major comeback.

Since January 2009, the stimulus package, supplemented by the federal fiscal budget for 2009 that President Obama has signed into law and his federal fiscal budget for 2010, that the US Congress is racing to enact, are setting the United States on a fiscal trajectory by which, even under optimistic projects about economic and revenue growth, the deficit will never again fall below the natural rate of growth of the economy. It has been decades, if not generations, since the fiscal viability of the Republic was cast into such doubt as it is today. The title of Buchanan and Wagner's 1977 book, *Democracy in Deficit*, suddenly has a ring of fresh, intense relevance.

It is comparatively easy, with the advantage of hindsight, to draw causal connections between the Federal Reserve's easy money policy in the last several years of Alan Greenspan's chairmanship, to rising personal indebtedness and the house price bubble; and between Chairman Ben Bernanke's sequence of interest rate hikes, from 2007 onwards, to the popping of the bubble, to debt-deflation and to a severe financial crisis. It is harder to analyze the economic effects of the fiscal deficits because, while economic theory tends to suggest that government borrowing should cause real interest rates to rise, this does not seem to happen empirically.

Our judgment on the role of debt in leading up to the crisis builds on the scholarship of James Buchanan (1957, 1958, 1964, 1966, 1969). Following a long line of classical economists, including Adam Smith (1776) and David Ricardo (1821), Buchanan argued that the burden of the debt falls on future generations. This view had been jettisoned by Keynesian economists during the early post-Second-World-War period, but rehabilitated, in a sophisticated form, by Buchanan in 1957. Buchanan's argument, as we shall show, uses the concept of "subjective cost analysis."

The most categorical rejection of classical doctrine on the debt burden issue came from Keynes's foremost disciple, Abba Lerner (1948). Lerner recognized that external borrowing does impose a burden on future generations, whose future consumption must be curtailed when the debt repayment comes due. However, he argued, there is no equivalent burden in the case of internal debt since "we owe it to ourselves" (Lerner 1948, 261):

If our children or grandchildren repay some of the national debt these payments will be made to our children and grandchildren and to nobody else. Taking them together they will be no more impoverished by making the payments than they will be enriched by receiving them (Lerner 1948, 256).

Lerner ignored the possibility that deficit-financed government expenditure might crowd out private investment. Government expenditure during a recession, in his judgment, was a free lunch. Even the additional taxes required to service the debt would be unlikely to deter future private investment. However, the leading Keynesian economist in the United States, Paul Samuelson, while generally endorsing Lerner's views, recognized that servicing the debt would distort private investment decisions and impose a deadweight cost on the economy (Samuelson 1948).

Buchanan (1969), dissatisfied with the Keynesian account, considers the public debt problem from the perspective of individual actors who collectively choose, through a democratic polity, both the level of government expenditures and the method of financing such expenditures. Buchanan distinguishes "choice-influencing (subjective) cost" from "choice-influenced cost" (and from objective cost). Choice-influencing cost has the following characteristics:

(i).   Choice-influencing cost is borne exclusively by those who choose; it cannot be shifted to others who do not make the choice;
(ii).   Choice-influencing cost is subjective, existing in the mind of each individual chooser, and nowhere else;
(iii). Choice-influencing cost is an *ex ante* concept, based on anticipations, not on retrospective calculation;
(iv).   Only the individual who is confronted with the choice can measure it;
(v).   Choice-influencing cost is dated at the moment of choice, and at no other point in time.

"Choice-influenced" costs (Buchanan, 1969) are the consequences that flow from the choices that are made. Choice-influenced cost does not reflect an evaluation of sacrificed alternatives since such alternatives are in the past. Thus, it does not represent opportunity cost. It is a future burden that emanates from current decisions. Choice-influenced cost may be experienced both by individuals who were party to the original choice and those who were not.

Buchanan (1969) argues that the ability to reduce the burden of choice-influencing costs by deficit financing, designed to push choice-influenced costs on to future generations, biases fiscal decisions in favor of increased government expenditures. Buchanan's subjective cost stands in contrast to the doctrine of "Ricardian-equivalence," the claim (Barro 1974) that "deficits do not matter" because they will be offset by increased saving to pay anticipated future taxes. In Buchanan's analysis, Ricardian-equivalence does not hold. Indeed, Ricardo himself did not believe that it held (Rowley, Shughart and Tollison, 2002). If Ricardian-equivalence held, all future costs would be choice-influencing.

Ricardian-equivalence, though a simple, extreme assumption that is often analytically useful as a point of departure, is implausible considering that all future costs include many futures when all of those alive to choose today will be dead. To Buchanan, then, deficit financing is, among other things, an expropriation of the wealth of future generations (who by definition do not vote today).

But how can the present generation expropriate future generations, when it is impossible physically to transfer goods backwards in time? While goods cannot be transferred backwards in time, the composition of production today can be altered, in favor of producing fewer investment goods and more consumption goods. In that case, future generations will inherit less capital and be poorer. A shift of resources from investment to consumption is a likely result of the failure of Ricardian-equivalence.

Some members of the population, foreseeing higher future taxes as a result of current deficits, may save and invest so as to smooth consumption over a future during which the government is likely to raise taxes to pay its debts. But others are either credit-constrained or (in the case of the elderly) do not expect to live long enough to be hit by the tax hikes. Such groups will rationally fail to save enough to offset the government's dis-saving (and others may fail to save because they are myopic), resulting in lower investment. The burden on future generations, then, is transmitted through a smaller inherited capital stock and a standing commitment to service or to repay the accumulated national debt.

This account of the economic effects of a national debt also suggests a reason why government borrowing might not raise interest rates. Interest rates are a function of the supply and demand for *loanable-funds*. Demand for loanable-funds comes from the government, from households, and from private entrepreneurs. The latter are individuals who have ideas, typically involving some degree of risk, for how to convert present resources into larger amounts of future resources. If they succeed, they will have to pay taxes on their gains. Taxes are asymmetric in that the government taxes the upside, but does not pay a corresponding compensation if the entrepreneur takes a loss, so they are especially burdensome for risky investments.

When government borrows, it absorbs some of the supply of loanable-funds, but at the same time, by creating expectations of higher future taxes, it makes risky investments less relatively attractive and thus induces a "flight to quality"—that is, to government bonds. The net effect on interest rates is indeterminate, but private investment surely falls.

The prediction of this account is that more government debt results in less private investment. This prediction is not falsified by recent US macroeconomic history. Private capital formation averaged just over 20 per cent of GDP from the end of the Second World War until the 1980s. It then fell, concurrently with the Reagan deficits, to a low of 17 per cent in 1991. Later in that decade, as deficits turned into surpluses and the real per capita federal debt began to fall, investment increased to almost 21 per cent of GDP. However, such investment declined under the Bush administration. Moreover, much of the investment that did occur in the George W. Bush years was in residential buildings, which now appears to have been very unproductive, but enjoying a politically privileged status because the US median voter is, or would like to be, a homeowner.

If government borrowing tends to suppress and distort investment, this explains why the strong "New Economy" productivity growth that pulsated through the economy during the fiscally conservative Clinton administration lost strength during Bush's first term and collapsed after 2005. This is one causal connection between the Bush administration's deficit spending and the late-2007 economic contraction.

3.8. AN EXPLOSION OF INTERVENTION: STIMULI, BANK BAILOUTS, FANNIE MAE AND FREDDIE MAC, TARP AND TALF

A distinctive feature of the present crisis is that the government and the Federal Reserve have intervened aggressively to "manage" the crisis from the beginning. Interventions have been carried out in unorthodox ways and on an unprecedented scale.

First, President Bush moved quickly, in concert with the Democrat-controlled Congress, to counter the economic contraction that began in December 2007. In February 2008, he signed into law a Keynesian fiscal stimulus package comprising $164 billion of income tax rebates directed at low- and middle-income American households. The *Internal Revenue Service* expedited delivery of those rebate checks to the relevant households in late April and early May 2008. Because these tax rebates were perceived by recipients to be transitory and not permanent, only 15 per cent was spent on household consumption (Posner 2009), the increased saving predictably denying the Bush administration its much desired economic stimulus.

The Bush initiative differed sharply from the early 2009 policy interventions of the Obama administration, in that it was composed entirely of tax cuts. Counter-recessionary public expenditure increases were not contemplated, other than through the automatic stabilizers. In any event, the economic contraction steadily picked up pace throughout the remainder of the Bush presidency.

In early October 2008, in response to the developing financial crisis, the Bush administration, with the support of the Democrat-controlled Congress, passed into law the *Emergency Economic Stabilization Act*. This legislation, pushed quickly through a reluctant (election preoccupied) Congress only by providing non-financial-crisis–related pork-benefits to Congress's key constituents, and by the tanking of the US stock market when an initial House vote rejected the Bill, established a program called the *Troubled Assets Relief Program* (TARP).

This Act funded Secretary of the Treasury Henry Paulson to purchase troubled assets (residential or commercial mortgages, and security obligations, or other instruments related to mortgages). He received an initial allocation of $250 billion, with the opportunity to access an additional $100 billion if the President certified need for it. An additional $350 billion could be accessed with the consent of Congress. The authority of the Treasury Secretary to spend these monies would terminate in December 2009.

Secretary Paulson diverted (possibly illegally) the first and the second tranches of TARP funding away from mortgage protection in order to support failing banks and collapsing automobile producers. These outlays were made without detailed conditions and essentially were wasted, not least in providing large bonuses to the very bankers who had created the crisis, in supporting the insolvent capital bases of seriously failing banks, and in propping up *General Motors* and *Chrysler*, two failing, rust-belt automobile producers saddled with untenable labor contracts and poorly designed automobiles. Early in 2009, President Bush requested and received the third, and so far final, tranche, on behalf of the incoming Obama administration.

The Bush administration left office with all its policy instruments, monetary as well as fiscal, relatively expansionist. As expected, the incoming administration would open the spigots of both policy instruments yet wider, trying to fulfill fiscally expansionist campaign promises, with old-fashioned Keynesian macroeconomics providing a false pretext for ideologically-driven political activism.

3.9. The Obama "stimulus" bill, and the new fiscal outlook

The Obama administration, in concert with a Democrat-led Congress and a compliant Federal Reserve, has deployed Keynesian monetary and fiscal policies designed to drag the US economy out of its financial crisis and economic contraction. Obama's domestic presidential reputation is now mortgaged (highly leveraged) to the success or failure of these interventions.

With respect to TARP outlays, the new administration is following the path finally decided upon by the Bush administration after a great deal of indecisive behavior by then-Treasury Secretary Henry Paulson. Only in late March 2009 did Treasury Secretary Timothy Geithner begin to clarify details of this program. Apparently, failing major banks will be propped up by leveraging the remaining $350 billion TARP monies with several trillion dollars of Fed-provided, FDIC-provided and privately supplemented financial support.

This program, announced in November 2008 but launched only in March 2009 - the Federal Reserve's *Term Asset-Backed Securities Loan Facility* (TALF) - has been presented as a crucial weapon in the battle to reverse credit contraction by financial institutions in the United States. According to the mission statement, the Federal Reserve will lend up to $1 trillion to buyers of top-rated securities, collateralized by credit-card debt, automobile debt, student loan debt, and small-business loans. TALF loans are *non-recourse,* meaning that the Federal Reserve has no rights to the borrowers' other assets, if they are not repaid.

The objective of this program is to leverage a relatively small input of private monies into a much larger total through a public-private partnership between the government on the one side and big-fund money managers, hedge funds, and insurers on the other, setting up a heavily subsidized competitive bidding auction for the toxic assets currently held by many banks.

By mid-June 2009, the response to this program has been miniscule, with financial institutions requesting only $6.4 billion of loans. The potential borrowers, particularly the hedge funds, are concerned that executive pay curbs on those receiving TARP monies will be extended to TALF participants, since the Treasury has pledged $100 billion to cushion the Federal Reserve from any losses. In addition, in part repayment for union campaign support, the Obama administration has placed restrictions on hiring foreigners on all participants in government programs, including the TALF.

In any event, the plan is likely to fall flat because of a lack of sellers, as well as because of a shortfall of buyers. For, in reality, many of the large banks holding toxic assets are insolvent rather than illiquid.

Many large banks are holding assets, especially whole loans, at values far below their market price, because, under accrual accounting, losses can be booked over several years. If toxic assets are sold at any price below the carrying value, banks would be forced to take a write-down and deplete levels of capital that are already dangerously low. Two-thirds of the Treasury scheme's purchasing power is directed to facilitating a market in toxic assets. Such a market is toxic to the continued existence of insolvent banks, unless they wish to be completely nationalized.

On average, America's largest ten banks hold one-third of their total assets in this form, for a total of $3.6 trillion. The carrying value of these assets was some 3 per cent above market price in December 2008, amounting to a total of $110 billion. If this becomes transparent, it will wipe out a quarter of these banks' tangible common equity (TCE) - their purest form of capital.

The remainder of the scheme's purchasing power will be directed at securities, which, at $3.7 trillion, comprise another third of the banks' assets. These are marked to market and are the main source of the savage write-downs that the banks have suffered. However, this market is deteriorating so fast that there is a growing concern about the Federal Reserve becoming saddled with hard-to-value securities if it has to take on collateral.

Moreover, the banks with the least capital almost certainly have valued their worst (level 3) assets far too generously. If they sell them at market prices to TALF-funded customers, their tangible common equity, once again, would be depleted. Level 3 assets account for approximately 16 per cent of the assets of the largest ten U.S. banks (*The Economist*, March 28, 2009, 83-84).

Predictably, the TARP program, bereft of any significant additional bank custom, is metastasizing in May 2009, like out-of-control cancer cells, into other areas of business enterprise. Specifically, several major insurance companies are now extending begging bowls to Treasury Secretary Geithner, who appears to be only too willing to throw a few taxpayer billions in their direction, in so doing, extending the grip of the Obama administration yet further over US private enterprise.

With respect to fiscal stimulus, the President drove through a compliant Congress, and signed into law on February 17, 2009 the *American Recovery and Reinvestment Act*. Its price tag of $787 billion makes this pork-laden Act the largest single government stimulation legislation in the history of the Republic. The legislation includes $288 billion (37 per cent) devoted to tax cuts. Another 18 per cent is devoted to state and local fiscal relief ($144 billion), and 45 per cent is devoted to federal social programs and federal spending programs ($357 billion).

Critics claim that a significant portion of the spending is not directed to job stimulation at all, that much of the potentially job-creating outlays are back-loaded and will not occur until late in 2010, when the economic contraction may be over. They further note that because the tax cuts are transient rather than permanent, they will be largely saved and not spent by recipient households, many of which fear future job losses or wage cuts.

Becker and Murphy (2009) correctly argue that there is no stimulus free lunch. Much of the stimulus package is directed to areas of relatively high employment (education and healthcare) and will simply divert resources from existing uses. Much of it is back-loaded and will not impact on the economy before the economic contraction is over. They estimate a multiplier well below one for the expenditure side of the fiscal package (Becker and Murphy 2009). New classical economists would expect a multiplier of zero to apply to such fully-anticipated fiscal outlays (Lucas 1975, 1976).

On February 18, 2009, President Obama revealed a $75 billion plan to stem the rising incidence of home foreclosures and repossessions. Approximately $50 billion will come from financial rescue funds already approved by Congress. These will be used to subsidize loan modifications between debtors and creditors (Reynolds 2009).

Together, the two dysfunctional mortgage corporations, *Fannie Mae and Freddie Mac*, seized by the federal government in September 2008, had received $60 billion of taxpayer monies by early April 2009 in a vain attempt to stem their mounting losses from toxic mortgage assets. There is every sign that the red ink in their profit and loss accounts is running ever more freely, fueled by these infusions of taxpayer dollars.

So dire are the prospects for these failed institutions that, on April 21, 2009, David Kellerman, the Acting Chief Financial Officer of *Freddie Mac*, with his quasi-governmental organization under investigation by the *Securities Exchange Commission* and the *Department of Justice*, with the Obama administration pressuring him not to disclose financial information concerning the true extent of *Freddie Mac's* losses, hanged himself in his basement at the age of only 41. Typical of this financial crisis, Kellerman had recently received a "retention bonus" of $850,000 as a reward for steering his organization full-speed onto the financial rocks.

Congress has passed and Obama has signed into law a 2009 budget with a $1.75 trillion deficit, loaded with 8,000 earmarks amounting to $8 billion. President Obama has recently presented to Congress a pork-laden 2010 budget proposal loaded with a $1.17 trillion deficit, and that calculated on extremely over-optimistic assumptions regarding economic recovery.

3.10. The Federal Reserve resorts to unorthodox methods

At the same time, the Federal Reserve lowered federal funds rates from 5.25 per cent in early 2007 to 0.25 per cent in late 2008. The Federal Reserve significantly increased the money supply (approximately doubling the size of its balance sheet) not only through regular open-market operations, but also by irregular operations that have expanded the range of assets held in its portfolio to include "relatively safe" corporate bonds and mortgage-backed securities.

More recklessly, the Federal Reserve has also extended sizeable credit lines to struggling financial institutions, as well as collaborating with the Treasury in creating public-private deals to encourage hedge funds and other financial institutions to purchase toxic assets (now euphemistically referred to as "legacy assets") from under-water clearing banks.

In essence, the Federal Reserve is debasing its own balance sheet trying to bail-out insolvent and illiquid banks in order to maintain an unsustainable structure of production. In doing so, the Federal Reserve is threatening the international reserve currency status of the U.S. dollar. As the quality of its assets continues to decline through the Term Asset-Backed Loan Facility (TALF), and as the equity ratio of the Federal Reserve's balance sheet has fallen from 4.5 per cent to 2 per cent, so its leverage has increased, dangerously, from 22 to 50. The Peoples Republic of China, the world's largest holder of US debt, is openly encouraging the emergence of a new international reserve currency (even a new international bancor currency) to replace the US dollar.

In a financial crisis largely caused by excessive leverage throughout the financial sector, it is foolhardy beyond belief for government to respond by excessively leveraging unsafe commercial assets within the balance sheet of its own central bank (Bagus and Schiml 2009). By its injections of credit into specific companies, the Federal Reserve is behaving as a political actor, and, as such, is exposing itself to vote-seeking political interventions from the legislative and executive branches of the U.S. government. In this respect, the Federal Reserve Chairman, Ben Bernanke may have irreparably compromised the future independence of the System that he serves.

3.11. President Obama's initiatives threaten the rule of law

FDR delayed until his second term before launching a direct assault on the United States Constitution. Barrack Obama rhetorically waded into the attack within the first 40 days of his first term, pursuing an opportunity created by his own administration. At issue were $165 million of bonuses paid out to past and present employees in January 2009 by the *American International Group* (AIG), a corporation that had recently swallowed $175 billion of TARP loans. The issue, much in the same manner as FDR's intervention, is whether contract law (however apparently egregious a particular contract) should be allowed to dominate ex-post regulatory opportunism.

Two agencies of the Obama administration, the Federal Reserve and the Treasury, were notified of AIG's decision well in advance of the payments (two months and two weeks respectively). The President was informed at least three days in advance. No government official objected to the payments until the news leaked to the general public.

Responding to a populist outcry, Obama demanded that the Congress should legislate to retrieve the bonuses retrospectively through targeted taxes levied at punitive rates on specified individuals. He urged the Congress to deliver "a final product that will serve as a strong signal to the executives who run these firms that such compensation will not be tolerated." (http://nytimes.com/2009/20/business/20bailout.html?ref=politics)

The House of Representatives approved by an overwhelming vote of 328-93 a bill that would impose retrospective 90 per cent levies on bonuses for traders, executives and bankers earning more than $250,000 per annum at companies holding at least $5 billion in bailout money. This implies that employees at 11 institutions - Citigroup, Bank of America, AIG, Wells Fargo, JP Morgan Chase, General Motors, Morgan Stanley, Goldman Sachs, PNG Financial, US Bancorp, GMAC, Fannie Mae and Freddie Mac - would face immediate tax penalties (Hulse and Herszenhorn 2009).

Legal analysts doubt whether the legislation would survive a court challenge, saying that it is tantamount to a retroactive "bill of attainder", which is banned by the Constitution. Of course, legal analysts expressed similar doubts about FDR's New Deal legislation, only to discover that, in 1937, five Supreme Court justices were prepared to violate their oaths of office to uphold the Constitution in response to powerful presidential duress (*West Coast Hotel v. Parrish*, 1937).

The US Senate wisely refused to enact the proposed legislation, serving as a much-needed brake on the President and the House. Inevitably, however, such an early threat to the integrity of the Constitution bodes ill for combating the pessimistic expectations that accompany any significant economic contraction. The public image of Congressman Barney Frank, wielding a populist "pitchfork" on the floor of the House of Representatives, egged on verbally by a newly-elected President, does not augur well for the future of capitalism in the United States.

On April 30, 2009, President Obama's apparent threat to the rule of law intensified. Thwarted by the corporation's bondholders in his attempt to prevent *Chrysler Corporation* from entering Chapter 11 bankruptcy reorganization, the President denounced the corporation's bondholders, referring to them as "vultures" because they insisted on maintaining their contractual rights as senior creditors. A number of the secured bondholders eventually backed down, unable to withstand the enormous pressure applied against them by the administration.

However, a number of senior bondholder creditors, including the State of Indiana, refused to acquiesce, and asked that the Chapter 11 proceedings should be set aside. Under strong pressure from the Obama administration, the US Court of Appeals for the Second Circuit allowed the reorganization to proceed. The US Supreme Court refused to grant *certiorari*, signaling that bondholders' prior rights are in jeopardy when the federal government has any stake in the bankrupty process. Thus, the assets of senior creditors of the *Chrysler Corporation* were plundered and partly redistributed to the United Auto Workers' Union (UAW), whose members had been largely responsible for bankrupting the company.

In June 2009, the Obama administration, placed a second government-owned *protégé* into Chapter 11 bankruptcy, this time *General Motors*. As with *Chrysler*, the secured bondholders are to be partially expropriated in favor of the UAW. Worse still, for free enterprise capitalism, the US Treasury Department will exercise a controlling interest (60 per cent) in the emerging corporation, with the power to appoint its directors and senior management and to control the vote on all matters brought before the remaining stockholders. This kind of public-private partnership once again breaches contract and securities laws. Worse still, it puts in place the apparatus that encourages the kind of corporatism characteristic of Italy under the dictatorship of Benito Mussolini.

3.12. CONCLUSION: KEYNESIAN MACROECONOMIC POLICIES AND IRRESPONSIBLE MICROECONOMIC POLICIES, 2001 – 2009: A FAILURE OF GOVERNMENT

Fiscal stimulus was applied by the Bush administration, as a limited response to the 2001-2 economic contraction. It may have provided some "stimulus" in the short run. But expansionary fiscal and monetary policy also helped precipitate the 2008 financial crisis.

In **Figure 8**, the solid line depicts the time path of real GDP per capita in the United States from 1929 to 2008. The dashed line, labeled "post-1968 trend" is derived by calculating the annual growth rate that would have raised GDP smoothly from its observed level in 1968 to its observed level in 2000. Defining a "trend" inevitably involves arbitrary cut-off dates, but we believe the trend shown is indicative of the economy's capacity.

The first thing to note is that the recession of 2001 was unusually shallow, with GDP per capita falling only 1.7% from 2000 to 2002. However, GDP per capita then grew below the trend line throughout the period 2001 to 2007, and the post-recessionary recovery phase lasted a relatively brief six years. The results of Keynesian stimulus after 2001 actually bear a slight resemblance to the 1933-37 experience: growth occurred, but remained below trend (though much less far below trend in 2001-07) and the upswing of the business cycle was unusually short. *Post hoc* does not necessarily imply *propter hoc*. Nevertheless, it does seem that the shallowness of the 2001 recession was purchased at the price of lower long-term growth and a truncated growth upturn to the business cycle.

Figure 8: The too-brief Keynesian recovery of the Bush years

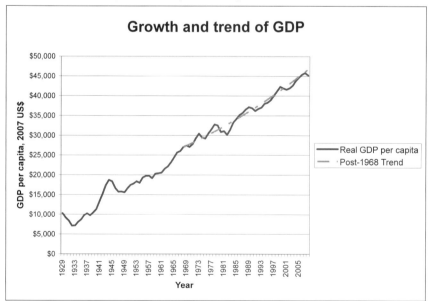

Source: BEA, Authors' calculations

This becomes more evident if we look at the behavior of the US macro-economy during the Bush presidency. What sustained the economy in 2001—rising house prices, residential construction, refinancing due to lower interest rates—proved to be the beginnings of the later disaster. The episode suggests that even if fiscal stimulus works, it does so only by postponing problems, which return later, in the manner of a new influenza virus, in a more virulent form.

If President Bush's fiscal stimulus policy truly was counter-productive in the medium run, it is very bad news that the Obama administration is pursuing fiscal stimulus on a far larger scale. The initiatives of Obama's first 150 days in office, taken together, imply an enormous increase in the long-term debt obligations of the federal government, a weighty additional burden on future generations.

The November 2008 elections placed into the Oval Office a liberal-democrat with the most left-wing voting record in the US Senate. The voting record was down-played throughout the electoral campaign. Since his election, however, President Obama has displayed his true colors through a policy program designed to shift the US economy sharply leftwards. Once this shift in economic policy is fully achieved, Anglo-Saxon *laissez-faire* political economy will give way to continental European social market political economy as reflected in current French and German economic stagnation.

The current economic contraction was brought about by a combination of policy failures by the various branches and agencies of the US government. The excessive monetary expansion of the Federal Reserve under the direction first of Greenspan and second of Bernanke closely mirrors the disastrous policy of the 1920s Federal Reserve under the leadership of Benjamin Strong, driving bubbles both in the stock market and in the housing market, especially in the form of sub-prime mortgages. The continuing fiscal deficits brokered between the White House and Capitol Hill throughout the period slowed down the growth rate of the economy and distorted resource allocation excessively into the construction of residential and commercial buildings.

Vote-seeking political actors, both in the White House and on Capitol Hill, pressured *Fannie Mae* and *Freddie Mac* to facilitate mortgages for low-income households that had no real prospect of paying their way. Lax regulation by the Federal Reserve, the FDIC and an alphabet soup of other government agencies allowed major FDIC-insured financial institutions to abuse their required tangible common equity (TCE) ratios and to engage excessively in high risk ventures. Tax laws that favor bonds over equity also encourage excessive corporate balance-sheet leverage.

Laissez-faire capitalism is not a free-for-all. It performs best under transparent, non-discretionary rules of the kind that evolved so efficiently in the United States over the period of the Great Moderation, 1980 to 2000, under the excellent economic governance provided by the administrations of Ronald Reagan, George H.W. Bush and Bill Clinton. Under the weaker economic governance of George W. Bush, the federal government and all its agencies largely ignored and flouted these rules of the game.

In such circumstances of regulatory failure, capitalism responded badly in several areas of economic activity (See Posner 2009, Poole 2009). Certainly capitalism bears some responsibility for the ensuing financial crisis. Let us be clear, however, that the fault does not lie primarily with capitalism. Profit-seeking impulses drive capitalist enterprise. It is the responsibility of government to ensure that these impulses are directed towards wealth creation. However competent the players on the field, a game without a functioning referee descends into chaos. Throughout President Bush's second term, the electorate should have yelled at him to "get back on the field, and get your hair out of your eyes, Ref!"

4

Laissez-Faire **Capitalism has not failed in The United States**

A particularly discouraging feature of the financial crisis of 2008 and its aftershocks is that a number of formerly free-market economists in the United States have, like Frank Knight during the 1930s, seemingly abandoned their intellectual stations and quit the battlefield, or have become apologists for social market economics (Posner 2009).

Where have all the flowers gone? Where now are all the new classical rational expectations and real business cycle scholars who once filled the economics journals with "the only game in town"? Where now are all the monetarists who once all-but-worshipped at the feet of Milton Friedman and rejoiced over the demise of hydraulic Keynesianism? Where now are all those efficient capital market theorists who once dominated the finance journals and saturated the major financial institutions? Where now are all those law-and-economics pioneers who once boasted about the wealth maximizing propensities of the common law? Where now are all those critics of economic regulation who so forcefully promoted late twentieth-century economic deregulation? Not all of them, surely, have gone to heaven, every one!

We will attempt to take the place of all those wilting free-market flowers, and briefly outline why the 2008 financial crisis and the associated economic contraction does not represent the failure of *laissez-faire* capitalism in the United States. In so doing, we fear that the Virginia and the Austrian Schools have now become the front-line shock troops in the defense of individual liberty and capitalism in the United States. The Chicago School, although still quietly supportive, has little fire in its belly following the retirements and deaths of the two leading 20th-century free-market economists, Friedrich von Hayek (1899-1992) and Milton Friedman (1912-2006).

4.1. *LAISSEZ-FAIRE* CAPITALISM VERSUS *STATE* CAPITALISM

First let us emphasize that, in distinguishing between *laissez-faire* capitalism and social markets throughout this monograph, we use the term *laissez-faire* only as a relative adjective. The United States has not enjoyed fully-fledged *laissez-faire* capitalism since the First World War.

Indeed, the only country that has enjoyed such status in living memory was the small British colony of Hong Kong before it became the Hong Kong Special Administrative Region of the People's Republic of China in 1997. For *laissez-faire* implies the existence only of a minimal state (Locke 1690) that serves primarily as a free market referee, enforcing the laws of property, contract and tort, while providing for the protection of its citizens against internal disorder and against external invasion.

By 2007, the United States economy, though more capitalist than any other major advanced nation, was already a heavily-regulated, mixed economy, with governments at national, state and local levels that engage in production, distribution, regulation and coercive wealth transfers, as well as serving as an often uneven-handed referee. We define such a system as *state* capitalist. In such circumstances, any failure must embrace both political and private markets, the issue being just where the balance lies.

4.2. HAS THE EFFICIENT CAPITAL MARKET HYPOTHESIS BEEN FALSIFIED BY THE FINANCIAL CRISIS?

Let us first suggest that the efficient-market hypothesis (EMH) did not fail in the United States over the period October 2007 to June 2009, as critics of the rational choice model from the standpoint of behavioral economics allege: at least not in any way that justifies a fundamental revision of its central role as a mechanism for the allocation of capital. Of course, the stock markets' extreme movements have understandably raised doubts. The Dow Jones Industrial Average peaked at 14,200 on October 9, 2007, fell to 9,600 on November 4, 2009, declined to an apparent bottom below 6,500 on March 6, 2009 and since then has risen to approximately 8750 in mid-June 2009. These shifts are far cries from the marginal changes typically associated with the behavior of the DJIA index. However, in our judgment, these facts can be explained without abandoning the EMH paradigm as long as EMH is defined from an Austrian economics perspective, in terms of dynamic rather than static criteria (Booth 2009, 30-31).

We use weak-form *dynamic* efficiency (in the Austrian sense) as the basis for our judgment. The basic postulates are that agents maximize expected utility; that on average the expectations of the population are correct in the long run;

and that agents update their expectations to account for new relevant information when it appears. EMH allows that some investors may over-react and others under-react to new information, but that such behavior is random and follows a normal distribution pattern.

Under weak-form dynamic efficiency, future prices cannot be predicted by analyzing past price data and excess returns cannot be earned in the long run by using investment strategies based on historical share prices or other historical data. Prices follow a random walk. Because efficiency is not instantaneous, sophisticated models may be able to exploit small short-term anomalies in the market, and to take advantage of market momentum as the market over- or under-shoots its equilibrium – hence the apparent successes of some hedge funds, brokers and investment banks during the early years of the twenty-first century. However, such returns typically are wiped out in the long run, as the market as a whole readjusts, as occurred late in 2008.

Stock market bubbles represent short run anomalies. Note, however, that individual agents remain rational throughout a bubble, recognizing the bubble itself, but unable to determine the peak or trough, which is determined through interactive trading. Posner (2009) correctly distinguishes, in this context, between risk and uncertainty in the sense of Frank Knight (1921). Risk, according to Knight (1921) can be calculated, either objectively or subjectively on the basis of past experience. No such probabilities can be attached to uncertainty, because of the absence of a relevant past.

During a stock market bubble, the turning point cannot be calculated objectively in terms of risk. The best predictor of the future is the immediate past. Many investors therefore rationally follow the trend (momentum) and continue to buy during the upturn, even borrowing money in order to buy on margin. For a variety of reasons, including inertia, and differing attitudes towards risk, some stockholders sell, clearing the market at each point in time.

Those who sell at or near the peak are lucky; those who are left holding stock as the bubble bursts are unlucky (unless they are able to hold on until the market recovers). The selloffs that follow are entirely rational, as would-be buyers and sellers scramble in a similar environment of uncertainty, some short-selling to take advantage of the market decline (momentum). If market volatility is high, risk-averse investors rationally diversify their stock portfolios, whereas gamblers rationally narrow their portfolios to focus on potential big winners. None of this is indicative of stock market inefficiency in the sense that we have defined it.

Those who criticize EMH typically follow the approach of Lange-Lerner in the socialist calculation debate (Booth 2009, 30). They argue, implicitly, that a socialist central planning authority (for the US, read the Federal Reserve) could determine efficient stock prices more efficiently than the market. They ignore the Austrian economics' insight that stock-market valuations reflect a continuous, decentralized process of information creation and assembly which simply cannot be replicated by a central planning body. A risk-averse, bureaucratic central authority could never adequately take into account the wide range of attitudes towards risk, or recognize and evaluate the opportunities for investment that commingle in a market economy, so as to substitute for the stock market as a means of allocating capital among diverse investments.

4.3. THE NATURE OF THE PRINCIPAL-AGENT PROBLEM IN FINANCIAL INSTITUTIONS

Let us now turn to the corporate boardroom to address the criticism against capitalism leveled by Richard Posner (2009) to the effect that a principal-agent problem between the shareholders and management of US financial institutions played a central role in generating the 2008 financial crisis. Specifically, it is charged that short-term personal wealth extraction on the part of management and traders exploited the rational ignorance of individual shareholders, and imposed long-term damage not only on the shareholders and bondholders of the financial institutions, but also (as a result of negative externalities) upon the broader US economy.

While there is, of course, some truth in this allegation the argument has been exaggerated by scholars such as Posner (2009), and by politicians such as President Obama and Congressman Barney Frank, who have reacted emotionally rather than rationally in their determination to identify a specific set of private market scapegoats on which to blame a complex economic misfortune.

From the outset, let us remember that we are analyzing and comparing real world institutions, not idealized forms of such institutions. Private markets are always flawed. Political markets are always flawed. What is important is that level playing field rules are strictly observed, as is the tradition of the Virginia School of political economy (Rowley 1993). Ours is not a world of private vice but public virtue, as John Kenneth Galbraith (1958) might have us believe; nor is it a world of private virtue but public vice, as Murray Rothbard (1962) might have us believe.

The most important institutional weakness of modern corporate capitalism, from the perspective of the principal-agent problem, is the widespread reliance on limited liability laws. These laws are provided by government. Limited liability truncates the downside risk for individual shareholders in a corporation, rendering vulnerable only the capital invested in the corporation, not total household assets, in the event of bankruptcy.

Limited liability is justified on the ground that it is a vehicle for bringing together large amounts of capital from diversified sources. But any measure that truncates down-side risk lowers the marginal degree of vigilance within the shareholder-principal class of a corporation. In this sense, the corporation typically is less well monitored than is its single-owner, unlimited liability predecessor. Attenuated downward monitoring predictably opens up avenues for opportunism among members of senior management within the corporation, especially under conditions of team-production (Alchian and Demsetz 1972), where individual marginal products cannot be identified.

Apologists for the corporate form of enterprise (Fama 1980) argue that effective checks against managerial opportunism still prevail. The threat and reality of takeovers supposedly constrain the ability of management to downgrade share values either by personal wealth extraction or by organizational inefficiency. The outside managerial market supposedly penalizes managers who divert their activities away from shareholders' longer-term interests, by lowering their market values. Upward and downward monitoring within the inside management class further checks opportunistic behavior.

Nonetheless, concentrated managements typically possess advantages over diffuse shareholders that may weaken accountability. For example, in the United States, state law significantly governs corporate behavior. In a "race to the bottom," the State of Delaware, through its statutes and court judgments, has made itself pre-eminent as the state that most protects management from shareholder/takeover and bankruptcy pressures. Predictably, a significant percentage of US corporations shelter management under Delaware laws.

An optimistic interpretation of this phenomenon is that it is "market-preserving federalism" in action (Weingast, 1995), and of course, investors could, if they wished, refuse to invest in firms headquartered in Delaware. But if it takes time for capital markets to learn all the ways that managements dodge accountability, large agency problems can appear in the short run. The information problem is exacerbated in the case of very large US financial institutions which are now viewed by the federal government as "too large to fail," because not only commercial but also political and regulatory factors affect future profitability.

In a complex and rapidly evolving commercial and political environment, awash with loose money, amidst the securitization of mortgages and the emergence of new, complex derivatives, the mortgage market being heavily distorted by subsidies and political support, it is not surprising that the forces of market discipline failed to keep pace with the threat of agency problems posed by stock options schemes, bonus bonanzas, and subprime lending. Regulators, it is important to note, did no better: every government regulatory agency was comatose at the wheel. The market chaos that ensued can be regarded as the outcome of rational behavior in a dysfunctional state capitalist environment.

4.4. The sources of moral failure

The moral indignation against financiers which has erupted in the past year is no doubt partly justified. But under *laissez-faire* capitalism, competitive market pressures constrain impulses to deviate from economic morality among those who produce, and those who exchange goods and services (Becker 1957). Political markets sometimes punish illicit sex on the part of politicians, but tend to exacerbate the kinds of moral failings that pose threats to the economic system.

The top of the pyramid of moral culpability for the 2008 crisis belongs to those politicians who, in coalition with the major financial institutions, encouraged individual citizens to spend well beyond their means, in order to support the bubble economy that emerged from the 2001-2 recession. Government policies, especially the distortions of the mortgage market outlined in Chapter 6 of this monograph, helped to send the message (which politicians gave financial institutions incentives to amplify): "No credit: no problem!" "Bad credit: even better!" "Use your stimulus benefits on a spending spree." "Whatever you do, *do not save*." Keynesian stimulus policies and mortgage subsidies created a climate of shallow, unsustainable prosperity which improved the short-run electoral prospects of politicians at the expense of the long-term health of the economy.

Close behind, further down the pyramid, are located those politicians, at all levels of government who banned financial institutions from discriminating among would be borrowers on the basis of economic criteria, when such criteria correlated with racial and/or ethnic characteristics (anti-red-lining legislation). These are the same politicians who pressured the regulatory authorities to lower financial standards for mortgages, to extend the myth of home-ownership to households who had no realistic means of repayment. "A rising market lifts all sinking vessels," was the slogan. But what happens when the market fails? They did not intend to be in office by then.

A little further down, are located the many regulators in the United States who sold out, either to the politicians, or to the financial institutions that they were supposed to regulate. The alphabet soup of such organizations is listed in detail in Chapter 6 of this monograph. In this section, we direct attention to four important federal regulatory bodies that have earned their memberships in the *Regulatory Hall of Shame*: the Federal Deposit Insurance Corporation, the Securities and Exchange Commission, Fannie Mae, and Freddie Mac.

On the lower rungs of the pyramid are located the inept senior management of large US financial institutions who destroyed their shareholders' wealth by investing in assets that they were incapable of valuing, in so doing leveraging their balance sheets to excessively high ratios, all this as a means of extracting large, unearned bonuses from their failing institutions. Their behavior was facilitated by government.

That said, we do not excuse private sector actors who put personal wealth accumulation ahead of their fiduciary responsibilities to shareholders and bond-holders, and whose irresponsibility and greed ultimately cost the US taxpayer and the US economy dearly. Unqualified endorsements of the virtues of self-ishness such as those of Ayn Rand (1957) are naïve in a world characterized by significant Pareto-relevant negative externalities, high transaction costs, and incomplete contracts.

At the lowest level on the pyramid are located all those US households who, with or without advice from mortgage lenders, realtors, credit card companies, and/or auto-dealers, cast aside any notion of budget balance as they rushed into debts that they never had any expectation of repaying. Not all of these households should be regarded merely as victims. They have imposed significant wealth losses on the honest, hard-working, financially prudent households that scrupulously balanced their budgets through the business cycle. Policies, such as those recently implemented by the Obama administration, designed to help reckless households to keep what they never really owned, are very unfair and create serious moral hazard problems for the future.

The policies of the US federal government and its agencies are at the heart of the moral failings that came to light in the course of the 2008 crisis. Even when the misdeeds occurred in the private sector, they were encouraged by the interventionist policies of the government, which in turn reflects the perverse incentives faced by politicians and presidents in a system where the government has grown too large. *State* capitalism rather than *laissez-faire* capitalism is the primary source of the moral failings which are now the object of populist anger that is being fueled, ironically, by the very politicians who were the chief culprits in stoking the house-price bubble that caused the financial crisis.

5

Public-Choice-Compatible Policy Recommendations

I n the present economic crisis, opponents of the bailouts and the "stimulus" plan are sometimes charged with being mere naysayers. For example, New York Times columnist David Brooks called the GOP's response to the crisis "unserious" (Brooks 2009).

To be fair, a dissenter who stands little chance of influencing policy may reasonably regard his time as better spent explaining what is wrong with the bad policies that are being enacted than dreaming up better ones that will not be. Also, it is quite legitimate to advocate doing nothing if all the policy responses that are feasible or politically possible would make matters worse. But it is important for the public to understand how a market-oriented response to the crisis, if pursued, would achieve the full recovery that the current government-driven policy program will probably prevent. It is also prudent to formulate market-oriented responses that are likely at some future point in time, to find favor with a majority of US voters.

That is not to say, however, that a politician who implemented the platform outlined here would necessarily improve his or her immediate chances of re-election. There is a disturbing possibility at present that the policies simply could not get majority support at a time when too much of the public is learning the wrong lessons from the crisis. It may be necessary to help (or wait for) people to learn the right lessons from the crisis before solving the problems of the US economy will become politically feasible.

Much of the advice we offer here is microeconomic, rather than macroeconomic, in nature. Micro policies do have macro-economic effects. For example, pro-growth micro policies are the main reason why the US economy performed so much better in the 1980s than in the 1930s, though both periods were characterized by tight money and deficit spending.

Where Roosevelt expanded unions' privileges, Reagan busted them. Where Roosevelt found new ways to micro-manage the economy, Reagan found ways to deregulate. Where Hoover signed, and Roosevelt maintained, the *Smoot-Hawley Tariff Act*, Reagan was an avowed free trader who initiated the *Uruguay Round* of trade negotiations that gave rise to the *World Trade Organization*. Where Hoover and Roosevelt maintained the draconian immigration laws of the 1920s, Reagan signed an amnesty for illegal immigrants.

Moreover, microeconomic advice is less subject to "model uncertainty" than macroeconomic advice. Whereas New Classical macroeconomists, Monetarists, Austrian economists, Keynesian economists, and New Keynesians macroeconomists may differ about whether or not counter-cyclical fiscal policy is useful, a large majority of economists agree that rent controls predictably cause housing shortages, and the vast majority of economists accept that "the country is made better off" by free trade. And so we advocate boosting housing demand through immigration reform; promoting job creation by defending and extending the right to work; and a unilateral suspension of all tariffs and trade barriers.

There is also one point of agreement between our recommendations and the policies currently being pursued: monetary policy. While inappropriately cheap money was a major cause of the crisis, it is greatly needed now, and we applaud the Federal Reserve's aggressive efforts to expand the money supply, especially the recent adoption of "quantitative easing" through open-market operations, despite the risk of medium-term inflation that this involves. We are strongly critical, however, of acquisitions by the Federal Reserve of private assets as part of its quantitative easing program, a policy that politicizes the Federal Reserve, encourages rent-seeking on the part of corporations, and downgrades the assets of the central bank (White 2009).

Yet it is true that much of our advice is negative: *do not* try to "stimulate" the economy through (more!) deficit spending; *do not* bail-out failing firms; do not embark on new regulatory efforts that restrict freedom of contract (though it *is* appropriate to attach more stringent conditions to FDIC deposit insurance). Our opposition to these policies is largely rooted in the "Virginia School" perspective on political economy.

The Virginia School tradition goes back to the scholarship of its founders, James M. Buchanan and Gordon Tullock, (Buchanan and Tullock 1962) and has been continued and expanded by such second-generation contributors as Peter Bernholz, Geoffrey Brennan, Roger Congleton, Charles Goetz, Henry Manne, Dennis Mueller, William A. Niskanen, Michael C. Munger, Mancur Olson, Charles Rowley, William F. Shughart II, Robert D. Tollison, and Richard E. Wagner (see Rowley and Schneider 2004). Most of the contributions are scientific in the form of positive public choice. However, the Virginia School has always contributed to moral philosophy and its practitioners are more than willing to participate in policy discussion.

The central insights of the Virginia school are (a) that all actors in politics and government are self-interested and therefore act very differently from the omniscient, benevolent, unitary "governments" or "social planners" that inhabit politically naïve economic models, and (b) that well designed constitutional rules are necessary to limit the damage from the perverse incentives that tend to pervade politics. At a time when the lines between public and private are being deliberately blurred, these insights are more urgent than ever.

5.1. MONETARY POLICY: QUANTITATIVE EASING

Monetary policy is one area where the response to the 2008 crisis has been the opposite of the disastrous response to the 1929 crisis (Meltzer 2009, O'Driscoll 2009, Schwartz 2009). Whereas the Federal Reserve in 1929-33 allowed the M2 money supply to fall by a third, in 2008 the Federal Reserve adopted a strongly expansionary posture and managed to expand M2 by over 10 per cent within the course of one year. The Federal Reserve has been engaged in "quantitative easing" since the fall of 2008, in part through the questionable means of buying bank bonds. On March 19, 2009, the Federal Reserve announced a plan to issue another $1.2 billion of money buying long-term Treasuries and mortgage debt. This is by far the main reason to expect that the US economy will recover, at least partially, and that the contraction beginning in 2008 will be far more benign than the Great Depression.

Clearly, monetary expansion on this scale creates a risk of inflation once economic recovery occurs and the income velocity of circulation of money returns to its normal range (Bagus and Schiml 2009, Bernanke 2009, Dowd 2009, Issing 2009, Melloan 2009, Samwick 2009). But this brings us back to asset prices and the question of how inflation is defined. If "price stability" were understood to include house prices, the Federal Reserve would have been faced with measured inflation above its preferred range throughout the period 2001-2006. Now, by contrast, with the post-2006 crash in house prices, a price index that included housing prices would have hovered near the deflation point as of late 2008 and by now would almost surely be registering substantial deflation.

Reports suggest that house prices have fallen by an average of 30% between the end of the second quarter of 2006 and June 2009. They still continue to fall. In view of such large house price drops, even a non-trivial rise in the CPI, such as the Federal Reserve's current monetary expansion eventually will provoke, if it impacts significantly on the housing market, could be interpreted as merely a shift in relative prices rather than true inflation.

We have argued earlier that Federal Reserve policy should try to prevent asset as well as consumer price inflation. We are not the first to do so. In 1999, worried *Economist* writers argued that:

> The consumer-price index is a flawed measure of inflation. Ideally, an effective measure should include not only the prices of goods and services consumed today, but also of those to be consumed tomorrow, since they, too, affect the value of money. Assets are claims on future services, so asset prices are a proxy for the prices of future consumption. (*The Economist,* "Hubble, bubble, asset-price trouble," 9/23/1999)

A tighter monetary policy by the Federal Reserve would probably have aborted the housing market bubble before it inflicted significant harm on the US economy. In hindsight, it seems clear that whatever harm might be thought to come from consumer price inflation and deflation, the harm of house-price inflation and (especially) deflation are at least as bad.

A revision of the price index to include house-prices would enable the Federal Reserve credibly to commit to some re-inflating of housing prices, but only as part of a general monetary policy of pulling the newly-constructed CPI out of deflation. Note that this proposal does not imply that the Federal Reserve should ever target the CPI for price inflation in excess of 2 per cent per annum. It simply redefines the CPI for this purpose, including house prices, instead of rental values, with an appropriate weight.

Of course, inflation is not a free lunch. During the past year, the Federal Reserve has approximately doubled its balance sheet through quantitative easing policies. If the income velocity of circulation of money recovers, the Federal Reserve will have to reabsorb much of the currency it has issued in order to prevent inflationary expectations from spinning out of control. This will drive up real interest rates, and may choke off the upturn of the business cycle and cause another recession. Such a strict monetary policy is essential if the Federal Reserve is to avoid a return to the stagflation policies of the 1970s.

For better or worse, in our system, it is the Federal Reserve's role to provide a currency, and ensure price and financial stability. In the absence of any recent experience with free banking systems, we can offer no workable substitute for this arrangement; but the Federal Reserve System involves serious dangers. Obscure technical mistakes can have devastating consequences-of which both the present crisis and that of the 1930s are examples. Another problem is that the Federal Reserve can become the victim of its own success. The more credibly the Federal Reserve is able to assure private markets of the stability of prices and the macro-economy, the more private markets will go "short on volatility," as households, firms, and banks leverage their assets and liabilities to maximize profits or smooth consumption.

While it is true that the current crisis in large part is the fault of the Federal Reserve, this is by no means because either Alan Greenspan or Ben Bernanke or their subordinates were or are corrupt. For the most part, the Federal Reserve, to date, has avoided the widespread corruption from campaign contributions that permeates the rest of the US political marketplace.

Rather, the strange role of the Federal Reserve, as an island of independent central planning in an (albeit diminishing) capitalist sea, is simply a very difficult one to play well, especially during periods of economic turbulence. However, as the Federal Reserve shifts outwards from its traditional role in controlling the supply of money, into the provision of select credit to ailing corporations, so it treads on more and more political toes, and exposes itself to the visible boot of politics.

The coincidence of the technically advisable course of monetary expansion with that which is favorable to the median voter mitigates threats to the independence of the Federal Reserve System in the short run. In future, the Federal Reserve will have to adopt less popular policies. At all cost, the Federal Reserve must steer clear from politics, in the tradition of Paul Volcker when he chaired the Federal Reserve; and wiped out price inflation in the United States, at the predictable cost of a recession similar in magnitude to that of 2007-9. Some thirty years on, he is now hallowed for his courage and wisdom.

5.2. RE-INFLATE HOUSING PRICES THROUGH IMMIGRATION REFORM

In the annals of human folly, there are probably few sadder spectacles than that of 19 million homes[4] standing empty in the US, thereby fueling an economic meltdown, while tens of millions of people beyond the US borders would be happy to move in, and work and live in them, but are prevented from doing so by the armed force of US border police.

Loosening the borders by relaxing immigration laws beyond current job-specialization and family-related levels, would directly reflate housing prices by increasing demand, thus attacking the very roots of the crisis. However, since an open borders policy with no strings attached is not politically realistic, given high transaction costs of assimilation, difficulties of preventing access to welfare

---

[3] http://moneynews.newsmax.com/streettalk/home_vacancy_rate/2009/02/04/178301.html

and other social benefits, etc., it is essential to make additional immigration pay its way.

An attractive policy is one of establishing large additional annual immigration green card slots and simply auctioning them off to the highest bidders, subject to anti-terrorist screening requirements. A supplementary policy, if credit-rationing is a deterrent to the full auction solution, is one of releasing large numbers of green card slots selectively, paying regard to the high occupational skills of applicants, and charging those who are successful annual fees until a predetermined aggregate transfer has been achieved. Immigration revenues could then finance annual wealth transfers to existing American citizens.

In this policy field, reliance alone on the potential compensation test will not work. Actual compensation is essential to overcome understandable resistance from those who will suffer short-term from an increased rate of immigration.

Immigrant households will help to stabilize house prices as they bring spending power to that market. They might do so either as buyers, or as renters, in which latter case a property's potential as a source of rental incomes would raise its market price. Many would bring capital and/or entrepreneurial abilities to establish new ventures, creating additional job opportunities.

The crackdown against illegal immigrants in the United States since 2006 helped to drive out hundreds of thousands of illegal immigrants, directly undermining house prices in certain regions. It should cease with immediate effect. Instead, Congress should pass some kind of amnesty, along the lines of the *Comprehensive Immigration Reform Act* that passed the Senate (but unfortunately died in the House of Representatives) in 2006.

5.3. Unilateral free trade: suspend all tariffs and trade barriers

In an attempt to spread economic recovery to the rest of the world, to benefit its own consumers and to lower the value of the dollar, this would be a good time for the United States government to introduce unilateral free trade, eliminating all tariffs, quotas and other constraints on the free entry of goods and services.

Of course, unilateral free trade is a textbook policy that economists have been advocating for more than two centuries, without curing special interest groups, politicians and presidents of their penchant for protectionism. Perhaps free trade is always a good idea; but is there any special reason to adopt free trade *now?*

There is. The most favorable interpretation that can be put on governments' perennial resistance to free trade is that governments recognize subtle reasons why certain sectional interests deserve favorable treatment even at the expense of a broader public that is burdened by additional, albeit opaque costs. At the present time, when economic pain is not restricted to particular regions or industries but is general, trade barriers are an expense the broader public should not be asked to afford.

Is it politically feasible to implement a policy that provides dispersed benefits at a significant level of concentrated costs, when those benefits significantly outweigh the costs? The *Repeal of the Corn Laws* in mid-nineteenth century Britain, by a Conservative Government heavily dependent on the votes of landowners, whose rents declined as corn prices fell, stands alone as an exceptional victory of this nature.

The Conservative Prime Minister and statesman, Sir Robert Peel, who successfully marshaled the legislation through the House of Commons, lost his position in the wake of the transition to a market economy. But his name is immortalized as a consequence of his personal sacrifice. Politicians do not make such sacrifices in the United States. There are no statesmen currently on the political horizon. As in the case of immigration reform, the application of limited compensation for those adversely affected by free trade is recommended as a vote-gathering mechanism.

5.4. LABOR MARKETS: EXTEND THE RIGHT TO WORK

The United States government should loosen up the job market by blocking legislation designed to strengthen labor unions, and curtailing the privileges unions already enjoy. A rise in union activism, made possible by the *Wagner Act* of 1935, was one of the main factors that kept unemployment so high during the Great Depression. The *Employee Free Choice* "card check" legislation that would take away the secret ballot in union elections, which unfortunately candidate Obama advocated on the presidential campaign trail, and which he is pursuing through legislative action, is a formula for a rerun of this grim scenario. Policy should move in the opposite direction by allowing employers to offer inducements to workers not to join unions, which they are forbidden to do under the *Taft-Hartley Act* of 1947.

Also, it would be useful, at least for the duration of the economic contraction, to suspend minimum wage laws. Microeconomic theory suggests that minimum wages cause unemployment. In fact, unemployment has increased, though not necessarily for that reason alone, since the Democratic Congress, with the acquiescence of President Bush, increased the minimum wage from $5.15 per hour to $5.85 in 2007, then to $6.55 in 2008; and it will rise again in 2009, to $7.25 per hour.

A minimum wage, by definition, deprives individuals of rights, specifically of the right to work for low wages. It consigns workers who cannot create more than $7.25 per hour worth of value in any job to unemployment. It also prevents workers from accepting jobs with low pay but large opportunities for human capital accumulation. In this time of crisis, workers should be allowed to find jobs any way they can.

Once again, changes in laws designed to provide disbursed benefits to the many at the cost of concentrated losses to the few will be difficult to enact. At the trough of a recession, however, policies that increase available jobs are valued more highly by the median voter than they are at the peak of a boom. Now, therefore, is the time to extend, not to eliminate, right-to-work laws

5.5. JUST SAY NO TO (CONVENTIONAL) FISCAL STIMULUS

When it comes to fiscal policy, our point of departure is a variation on the "first do no harm" principle of the *Hippocratic Oath*; namely, we suggest the government should not embark on policies that exacerbate the economy's major problems. Since one of those major problems in the United States is a bloated and still burgeoning national debt, we endorse no stimulus that increases the size of the national debt. In the absence of offsetting tax increases, that means no fiscal stimulus at all, save through automatic stabilizers; though it turns out there is one clever way to provide a form of fiscal stimulus without growing the debt.

New classical economists (Lucas 1975, 1976) argue that fiscal stimulus cannot work because it is funded by borrowing, which absorbs money that would otherwise have gone to private investment. Keynesian bloggers like De Long and Krugman now greet that argument with outrage, responding basically that it fails to take unemployment into account. These critics have in mind a Keynesian alternative model with fiscal multipliers, in which new government activity does not crowd out private-sector activity.

This dispute illustrates the problem of "model uncertainty": economists disagree on what to recommend because they do not know what economic model (if any) best describes the real world. However, we can develop a simple but convincing model that captures the point about crowding-out while still taking unemployment into account.

Let us first assume that some resources are unemployed, and that a public-spirited government tries to mobilize these resources by creating public-sector jobs on projects with significant value-added–in short, a scenario that is a typical point of departure for Keynesian fiscal stimulus prescriptions. Next, assume that good government projects, which create real value-added, typically require quite specific skill sets which are unlikely to correspond precisely to those of the local unemployed.

When the government creates jobs, it cannot guarantee that those jobs go to people who would have been unemployed. Realistically, we also assume that government programs operate at a lower efficiency, specifically 80 per cent, of private programs, because of the absence of price signals and market discipline, and the presence of bureaucratic obstacles (Niskanen 1971).

Who gets stimulus jobs? The unemployed may be the most motivated to apply, but they probably also have less useful or less tightly-honed skills, while the employed, or more precisely, those who would have been employed in the absence of stimulus, may want to move into government jobs if the latter offer better pay, or better job security, or require less effort. We shall assume that these counter-effects cancel out, and that those who become employed in stimulus jobs are randomly drawn from the general employable population. **Figure 9** shows what happens in the model.

Figure 9: Employment creation, and crowding out, and diminishing returns to stimulus

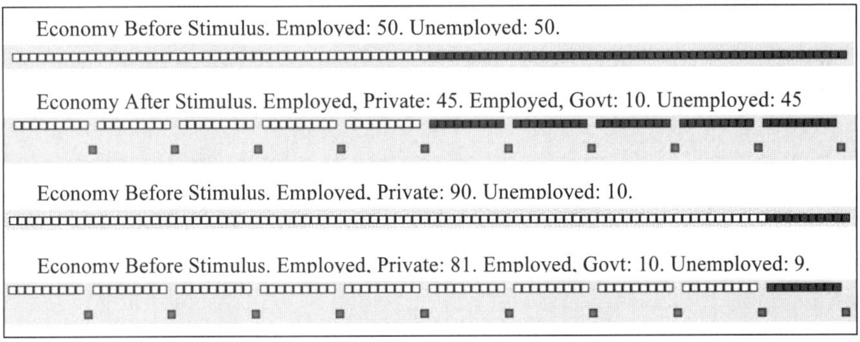

In Figure 9, the labor force is represented as a row of small squares. White squares represent workers employed in the private sector, dark squares represent unemployed workers and dark squares below each row represent workers employed in a government stimulus program.

The first row represents an economy with 50 per cent unemployment. The second row shows the effect of a job-creating program that employs 10 per cent of the work force, or 10 workers, half formerly unemployed, and half formerly employed in the private sector. Suppose that each worker in the private sector produces $100, and each worker in the government program produces $80. In such circumstances the stimulus raises GDP from $5,000 to $5,300. The fiscal multiplier (to use a Keynesian term) is 0.6. The third and fourth rows represent a scenario in which the initial rate of unemployment is only 10 per cent. In this case, nine of the stimulus workers will be drawn from the private sector and only one from the pool of unemployed. Pre-stimulus GDP is $9,000 and post-stimulus GDP is only $8,820. The multiplier is -0.12.

The specific numbers are merely illustrative, and should be given no particular weight. What matters is the general conclusion, namely that government job creation might serve as a "stimulus" to GDP in truly high-unemployment environments, but reduce GDP in low or moderate unemployment environments, by crowding out private-sector activity. In mid-June 2009, the rate of unemployment in the United States hovers around 9.4 per cent and is expected to peak at no more than 10.5 per cent, far below the levels of the Great Depression. Even if a fiscal stimulus could increase GDP in 1933, our model suggests that it is far less likely to do so in 2009.

The major insight that the tradition of the Virginia School would add to this analysis is that any private benefits created by stimulus spending will be dissipated, at least to some extent, by the *rent-seeking* activities that they induce. This will alter the nature of "stimulus" packages, ensuring that they will contain a great deal of earmarks directed by the political actors to favored constituents, which may be economically indefensible, but politically unavoidable from the perspective of politicians trying to stimulate the economy.

For example, in the recent 2009 "stimulus" bill, only $90 billion or so was on infrastructure and business tax cuts that might stimulate the economy, while most of the spending was targeted to appease long-standing political interest groups. Meanwhile, the entire expenditure package will attract rent-seekers: state and local agencies prepared to destroy their own resources in order to become eligible for federal funds and willing to deploy wasteful lobbying to secure as much of the rent booty as they can (Tullock 1967). In the limit, such competitive rent-seeking may dissipate in social waste an amount equal in value to the entire expenditure stimulus package (Tullock 1980).

Ultimately, while we think that the above arguments shed light on the effects of fiscal stimulus, the deeper point is simply that plausible ways of thinking about spending during a recession suggest that it will not stimulate GDP at all but, on the contrary, will simply cause waste and reduce the long-term rate of growth of the economy. A limited amount of "stimulus" will be provided by "automatic stabilizers," as falling revenues and the continuing costs of government services increase the deficit. Beyond that, we recommend no recession-based spending increases (temporary or permanent) in response to the current recession.

We additionally do not favor temporary tax cuts as an economic stimulant. Households are now aware that their excess expenditures and rising indebtedness have placed them in economic danger. Temporary tax cuts will not enter into permanent income and, therefore, will barely stimulate consumption (Friedman 1957). Only 15 percent of the President Bush's 2008 temporary tax cuts found their way into consumption expenditures. Far less than this predictably will be expended from the 2009-10 temporary tax cuts, given the increased gravity of household budgets. Long-term tax reform is a different story, but falls outside the scope of this monograph.

5.6. SOCIAL SECURITY REFORM

There is one way that the government could provide something like a fiscal stimulus *without* increasing the deficit. Among the government's liabilities are obligations to pay benefits to today's workers after their retirement, through the Social Security program. Social Security is *not* a social safety net: not only are benefits paid out to affluent individuals, but since benefit levels partly reflect lifetime earnings, and since the more affluent tend to live longer, they receive *more* Social Security benefits than the less well-off. African American men, because of their shorter life-spans, on average receive no Social Security benefits at all.

It would be morally unproblematic to allow these people to surrender some of their claims to future incomes from the government, in return for government bonds, and/or Treasury Bills, appropriately valued (this would involve actuarial calculations about the likely future stream of benefits, converted into government bonds of the same net present value). These government bonds would not be at the personal disposal of participants in the program; rather, they would be deposited in private Social Security accounts, to which participants would have access only after retirement.

Individuals could, however, instruct the managers of these private accounts to sell the government bonds in return for stocks. Stocks, which are volatile in the short run, but (despite the current collapse) out-perform other assets in the long run, are the ideal assets for long-term retirement portfolios; and the opportunity to convert promises of future Social Security benefits into stocks would likely be attractive to many, even if the terms of the conversion were not particularly favorable.

The government bonds sold from private Social Security accounts would then be made available to investors, among whom there is currently a ravenous demand for "flight to safety." We believe a program of this kind could provide a large and effective fiscal stimulus without increasing the burden of the debt.

The *Social Security Trust Fund* does not exist and the current *Ponzi* scheme, in which retirees are paid through the ongoing contributions of those in employment, is on the point of collapse, as the ratio of retirees to workers continues to increase. Therefore, major pullbacks from entitlement commitments are inescapable in order to keep paying future benefits without large tax hikes.

The government should lift the retirement age to 70, to reflect increasing life-expectancy, and should progressively restrict benefits so that high-end benefits increase at the rate of inflation rather than wage growth. These pullbacks from entitlement commitments ideally would occur simultaneously with the creation of a private account option, to avoid letting people cash out long-term commitments that are unaffordable, and would be part of a wider plan to bring the government budget into long-term balance.

5.7. Establish a plan for long-term budget balance

The Virginia School has a long association with the idea that democracy has an inherent bias towards deficit spending which needs to be corrected through constitutional rules. Buchanan and Wagner (1978) question whether, politicians' electoral interests being what they are, democracies can in practice be trusted to use the fiscal discretion to engage in peacetime deficit spending appropriately. Instead, they support a balanced-budget amendment to the United States Constitution as a means of making the social contract reflect the interests of future generations. Buchanan also believes the effect of such an amendment would be to restrict the size of government below levels that voters support when they can do so through (subjectively) "cheap" deficit financing (Buchanan 1967).

At a time when President Obama's fiscal policies are placing the fiscal viability of the United States government in doubt as never before, Buchanan's arguments are compelling. Any constitutional rule designed to balance the federal budget would need to bring the government's unfunded long-term liabilities, particularly the Social Security, Medicare and Medicaid entitlements, onto the balance sheet. To prevent the constitutional amendment from encouraging politicians to increase taxes, the rule should be complemented by a twenty percent of GDP income tax revenue ceiling.

For decades, a two-third dispersed majority within the US electorate has expressed a desire for a balanced-budget constitutional amendment. What has been lacking is political will, in the teeth of concentrated special interest group resistance.

5.8. Use the bankruptcy code to deal with failing automobile corporations

An economic contraction always involves an increase in the number of corporations that become bankrupt. Up to a point, this spike consists of healthy "creative destruction," as the market cleanses itself from waste and bad business practices that occur and accumulate during the prior upswing of the business cycle. Perspicacious corporations, as well as their counterparties, survive because they protect themselves from just such potential crises, while more reckless organizations are bankrupted. Thus the likely effect of a mild or moderate recession is to improve the average quality of those that remain in business.

Of course, in normal times it is not efficient to sit on a lot of extra cash, and the market rewards the same leverage that is fatal in a downturn. So in an abnormally deep downturn, some of the firms that go under may be responsible and efficient firms that took sensible risks and fell victim to extreme and unforeseeable events.

This is one reason why, while normal recessions improve the long-term efficiency of an economy, deep downturns are more likely to lower it. Inevitably, the counterparties of firms that go bankrupt also suffer during this process as their linkages with failed companies impose stress on their own viability. The perception, sometimes correct, that some companies are failing through mere bad luck, creates a political temptation to intervene to support them. But if government invades this market process, by providing outright subsidies or below-market loans to failing institutions, a number of downside risks follow.

First, tax dollars may be dissipated unsuccessfully, with non-viable companies surviving a few months longer before they finally collapse. Second, tax dollars may succeed in under-girding poorly organized companies, dissuading them from effective reorganization, leaving them too marginal to provide any real market contribution. Third, government subsidies may provoke moral hazard, signaling to the market as a whole that excessive risk-taking will not be punished when it fails, but will be rewarded when it succeeds. Fourth, subsidizing failing firms may breach the rule of law[5], by providing unfair trading advantages for some firms over others, and by breaching international trade treaties.

Furthermore, public choice consequences inevitably follow from government bail-out programs. Of course, both the executive branch, including the Department of the Treasury, and the Congress are already heavily politicized. However, the more they intervene, or threaten to intervene in specific markets, the greater the volume of rents that they hand out, or threaten to recall, the more focused and concentrated will be the rent-seeking/rent-protection pressures from those who compete for their favors. The wasteful consequences of such rent-seeking can be far-reaching and subtle, as all of a company's decisions become infected by the motive of courting political patrons rather than serving the customer.

It is instructive to analyze recent government bail-out interventions with respect to the US automobile industry through the lens of public choice analysis.

Two of the three major US automobile corporations, *General Motors* and *Chrysler*, have been slowly failing for a long time. As a consequence of poor management, unattractive auto designs, and ruinous labor contracts negotiated with the *United Auto Workers*, these corporations have steadily lost market share to foreign owned automakers, some of which operate factories in the United States. The three major US auto producers are barely viable during the upturn of the business cycle. During an economic contraction, they fail the market test.

In recent months, the Bush and Obama administrations have tried to bail out *General Motors* and *Chrysler* by a succession of multi-billion dollar loans. These bailouts were economically misguided and, throughout most of the country, politically unpopular. But of course, the opposite policy, to let *General Motors* and *Chrysler* go bankrupt, was highly unpopular in Michigan, where the issue is naturally more politically salient than elsewhere.

Auto-bailouts, then, are a classic case of "concentrated benefits and diffused costs" (Olson, 1965). On the one hand, lobbying monies are flooding into the campaign coffers of key members of Congress, and the State of Michigan is

---

[5] The reluctant decision made on April 30, 2009 to place Chrysler into Chapter 11 bankruptcy is a good example. The government attempted to use the large bank bondholders of Chrysler to trample the small bondholders and hedge funds into taking pennies on the dollar to avoid bankruptcy, while leaving the UAW in a much more privileged position. The government evidenced public anger when its bullying behavior was resisted, justifiably, by small creditors who stand to obtain a better deal from any bankruptcy court than from President Obama's union-obligated administration. The same bullying has occurred with respect to GM bondholders as GM moved into Chapter 11 bankruptcy on June 1, 2009.

strategically important in the 2012 Electoral College. On the other hand, nationally, there are far more losers than winners from an auto-bailout. The question was: can dispersed taxpayer anger offset these concentrated pressures? The answer was: no.

The right place for *General Motors* and *Chrysler* was always Chapter 11 bankruptcy, where, if they wished to emerge intact, they could reorganize, by trying to restructure labor contracts, completely replace their boards of directors and senior management, and slim down and reshape their product lines for the limited markets that they are now capable of reaching. If they failed in this endeavor, then they would have been liquidated, and their assets disposed of in a fire-sale, picked up, perhaps by European auto makers, notably in the case of *Chrysler*, by *Fiat*, or by such Japanese and South Korean companies as *Toyota*, *Honda* or *Hyundai*, and reorganized under foreign management to make profitable vehicles under realistic labor contracts. The final solution, of course, is the disappearance of these companies. The US government had no justifiable role to play in this process.

The auto-bailout is difficult to reject politically but easy to reject economically, since the failure of one or two major auto firms would not have a decisive impact on the US economy as a whole. The high price of the political solution becomes apparent when a United States President creates an auto task force, bereft of any previous experience in the auto industry, commissioned to report to National Economic Advisor, Lawrence Summers and Secretary of the Treasury, Timothy Geithner, neither of whom have any significant experience in for-profit organizations.

The outcome, where President Obama, whose only private market experience is a one year business consultancy, essentially assumed personal control over *General Motors* and *Chrysler*, firing their senior management and replacing their boards of directors and negotiating terms for their acquisition, reflects an extension of political discretion reminiscent of Soviet economic policy or of the Italian dictator, Benito Mussolini's corporate state.

Such extensions of political power do not portend future economic success. Nor are they harbingers of an early return to *laissez-faire* capitalism in the United States (*The Economist*, May 9, 2009, 14).

5.9. HOW BEST TO DEAL WITH FAILING BANKS: NO BAIL-OUTS, NO NATIONALIZATION

Failing banks and other financial institutions pose more generalized problems for policy-makers because their collapse reaches out broadly across the real economy. Payment systems and working and investment capital are essential to every industry every day, and bank failures probably played a major role in deepening the Great Depression. This was a key insight by the now-Federal Reserve Chairman Ben Bernanke when he was an academic.

Bernanke (1983) argues that the depth of the Great Depression is explained in part by the way bank failures increased the "cost of credit intermediation." Bernanke's hypothesis is that "the real services performed by the banking system is the differentiation between good and bad borrowers ... including screening, monitoring, and accounting costs, as well as expected losses inflicted by bad borrowers." The wave of bank failures led to a "rapid switch away from the banks [which] (given the banks' accumulated expertise, information, and customer relationships) no doubt impaired financial efficiency and raised the [cost of credit intermediation]" (Bernanke 1983, 263-4).

The temptation is for government to rush in to shore up such institutions through massive injections of taxpayer-provided liquidity, in the limit nationalizing those that are completely insolvent (Krugman 2009, Solow 2009). Not surprisingly, this view of the historical lessons of the Great Depression has affected the policy conduct of the Federal Reserve under Bernanke's leadership, as well as the US Treasury with which the Federal Reserve has worked closely (almost certainly too closely for the latter's political independence) since September 2008.

Desperate to prevent a systemic failure of the financial sector, the Federal Reserve and the US Treasury have intervened to prevent the bankruptcy of several major banks, including the *Citicorp Group* and the *Bank of America*, as well as such large financial institutions as, *Bear Stearns, Merrill Lynch, AIG*, and others, and to impose the outright nationalization of *Freddie Mac* and *Fannie Mae*, all at the expense of hundreds of billions of dollars in taxpayer money. In our judgment, this is a simply dreadful policy response fraught with political and economic danger.

We have already outlined the problems of allowing politicians to play election games with the US auto industry. The economic risks are far greater with respect to the financial sector, simply because the implications for resource misallocation are orders of magnitude greater (Cecchetti 2009, Congdon 2009, Dowd 2009, Lanman 2009, Miron 2009, Samwick 2009).

The political consequences are yet more disastrous when independent agencies like the Federal Reserve and the FDIC are drawn into the situation. As widely respected government agencies, that typically maintain a healthy distance from the political market, exercise more and more discretionary power and differentially affect private interests, they expose themselves to much greater po-litical pressure from Congress, from the executive branch, which appoints their members, and from outside rent-seekers.

The seven members that comprise the Board of Governors of the Federal Reserve are appointed by the President and confirmed by the Senate for stag-gered 14 year terms. There are two vacancies in June 2009. President Obama no doubt will appoint individuals politically sympathetic to his (and the Demo-crat-controlled Congress's) style of quantitative easing, rather than independent thinkers. Suggestions are currently being floated that the 12 Reserve Bank presi-dents, who are not confirmed by Congress, should lose their say over monetary policy (*The Economist* May 9, 2009, 18). President Obama has not used any of his frequent public speeches to bat away such suggestions.

A loss of independence by the Federal Reserve System will surely lead to higher inflation, as politicians seek the short-run gains of monetary expansion while ignoring economic costs falling beyond the horizon of political account-ability. Worse still, a politicized central bank constitutes an ongoing threat to the rule of law. Countries with politicized central banks are almost always char-acterized by low rates of economic growth, high rates of inflation and high levels of unemployment, as well as massive levels of corruption.

The result has been to trap the US government, and the taxpayers, in a los-ing game against potentially failing banks from a position of significant informa-tion asymmetry. **Figure 10** illustrates the nature of the problem.

Figure 10: Signal corruption: the price of bailouts

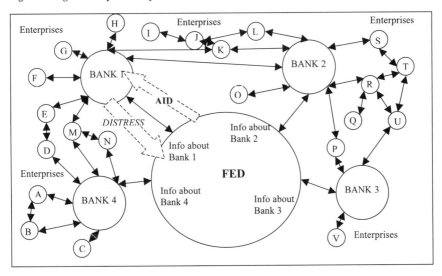

In Figure 10, each of the two-sided arrows represents a business relationship, involving transfers of money and information. There are four banks and an alphabet soup of enterprises. At the center of the network is the Federal Reserve, which possesses information about all four of the banks. This information provides the basis for its decision making.

In Figure 10, not all enterprises are connected to the banks directly. Firm T, for example, is unconnected. Even those who are unconnected depend on the banks indirectly because they are linked to firms that do business with the banks. For example, firm T does business with firms R, S and U, all of which are linked to banks. Some banks, for example Bank 1 and Bank 2, do business with each other. Some firms, for example, Firm M, do business with more than one bank.

Figure 10 serves as a visual to illustrate the concept of "contagion". Suppose that Bank 1 goes bankrupt. Firms E, F, G, H, K, and M do business with Bank 1. Most of these, perhaps, are borrowers, maybe one of them is an investment bank, which owns Bank 1's shares, or has lent money to it. If Bank 1 goes under, it will be unable to lend, its shares will fall to zero in value, and it will default on some debt. Firms that rely on it for their capital needs will be strapped for cash, and may fail themselves.

This in turn affects those with whom they do business. Bank 2 is directly exposed to Bank 1. Firm G is relatively healthy and would like to expand. It is well-known by Bank 1, which is no longer there. It must approach another bank with which it has no previous relationship. Bank 2 is willing to lend but demands collateral, which Firm G cannot provide because its assets have fallen in value in the economic contraction. The web-like nature of these interactions is easy to visualize in a full-information environment.

Recognizing that some such web exists, the Federal Reserve may decide that Bank 1 (think Citigroup, Bank of America, Wells Fargo, or GMAC) is "too big to fail" and might move in to provide a rescue. However, the Federal Reserve does not possess anything close to full knowledge about the nature and extent of Bank 1's entanglements, or the likely degree of contagion should the bank fail. Moreover, Bank 1 will have provided most of the information available to the Federal Reserve. Very powerful incentives are in place for Bank 1 to manipulate information flows beneficial to itself.

For example, if the number of entanglements is the route to its survival, Bank 1 will make sure that it is doing business with as many other banks and firms as possible in order to make its failure yet more catastrophic. If solvency is the criterion, insolvent banks will cook the books to make it look that all they require is a little liquidity (and then will attempt to manipulate the terms on which this is provided so as to obtain a subsidy that will put them back into the black).

This is why central planning works better in the very short run than in the longer term. Initially, a central planner (the newly-politicized Federal Reserve) can use information reported to the center from various actors in the decentralized system as the basis for its decisions. But when it starts to do so, it creates incentives for those agents to mis-report. Thus any signal that the central planner uses, or is expected to use, as a basis for decision becomes corrupted.

Given this inescapable problem, in our judgment, the appropriate policy with respect to the financial sector crisis is for the Federal Reserve, and the FDIC to step back and use their traditional instruments while the Department of the Treasury exits the scene[6]. Given the importance of this recommendation, let us briefly outline the nature of the traditional interactions between the central bank and the FDIC on the one hand, and struggling commercial banks and other FDIC insured financial institutions on the other.

Let us first distinguish between clearing banks (banks that take deposits and engage in check clearing and payment settlements) and other types of institutions, such as savings banks and mortgage corporations, organizations that take deposits, but do not engage in clearing and settlements (Congdon 2009). The former are much more attractive prospects for central bank support, because they have accounts with the central bank and remain under closer scrutiny by the central bank. The latter are a motley group that the central bank may view with varying degrees of suspicion.

Let us next distinguish between solvent and insolvent banks (Congdon 2009). A solvent bank enjoys an excess of assets over non-equity liabilities, whereas an insolvent bank does not. Clearly, solvent banks are much more attractive candidates for central bank support than insolvent banks. Insolvent banks typically do not justify central bank support of any kind.

Finally, let us distinguish between liquid banks, that hold some cash, either in the vaults, or in the cash reserve at the central bank, and illiquid banks that do not. Evidently, illiquid banks are more likely to fail than liquid banks, but they may remain solvent in the sense defined above. Illiquid banks, as long as they remain solvent, may merit central bank support under specified penalty conditions, typically as lender of last resort.

---

[6]Timothy Geithner is a less than inspired choice for the position of Treasury Secretary during a period of financial crisis. The idea that Secretary Geithner is capable of controlling the gaming behavior of 19 large US banks is simply not credible.

If it is agreed that, during a crisis, the most fitting recipients of lender-of-last-resort lending are solvent, though illiquid, deposit-taking, clearing banks, the question arises, under what terms? The answer provided by Walter Bagehot (1873) and summarized by Congdon (2009) is "in a run the central bank should lend cash to a solvent but illiquid bank at a penalty rate to whatever extent is necessary, as long as the loan is secured by good collateral" (Congdon 2009, 95). By inference, it should lend nothing to any other financial institution.

What then should happen to insolvent banks and other financial institutions? For all the public choice reasons advanced above, nationalization is not the appropriate solution. Government ownership of the banking system represents an enormous step towards corporatism, and threatens to impose enormous resource misallocation throughout the real economy. Well organized bankruptcy is by far the best solution to bank insolvencies (Buiter 2009, Congdon 2009, Goodhart 2009, Miron 2009, Romer, P. 2009).

For those operating with FDIC protection, the FDIC is the appropriate agency to process the liquidations and reorganizations, selling off the failing bank to a competitor, where such a deal is possible, otherwise paying off depositors quickly so that they can move their deposits to safe banks, while allowing other institutions to cherry-pick among the assets. If bank assets are insufficient to cover liabilities *other than* FDIC-insured deposits, losses should be borne first by the shareholders, then by the unsecured creditors, and last by the secured creditors of the banks, irrespective of relative political influence.

For those operating without FDIC insurance protection, the regular bankruptcy courts should be utilized to reorganize or to liquidate the offending institutions. Throughout, the Federal Reserve can ensure that the M2 money supply is undiminished through vigorous quantitative easing, as discussed above, encouraging the swift emergence of new credit-worthy banks to replace the failures that exit the market-place.

The alternative policy pursued by the Obama administration poses a serious threat to the political independence of the banking system. Of the nineteen major US banks subjected to stress testing in April/May 2009, four have been found clearly wanting, namely the *Bank of America, Citigroup, Wells Fargo* and *GMAC*. These four banks are already major recipients of TARP capital currently in the form of preferred stock.

An additional six banks are deemed through the stress tests to hold inadequate levels of tangible common equity, and will be expected to raise this through financial markets. In total, the stress tests require the banks to inject an additional $75 billion into tangible common equity.

The stress tests appear to have been rigged to present a false image of large bank solvency. Specifically, the buffer required for banks to absorb projected losses is far too lax (*The Economist* May 26, 2009, 81). The tests state that the banks' core capital (defined as tier-one common) should be at least 4 per cent of risk-weighted assets (which equates to 2.7 per cent of their total assets). This is below the level actually achieved in the middle of the financial crisis at the end of 2008 (5 per cent of risk-weighted assets) and well below the level achieved by the strongest banks globally (above 8 per cent of risk-weighted assets)). In 1929, when the financial crisis that led to the Great Depression started, the average tier-one common capital of US commercial banks as a percentage of risk-weighted assets was 13 per cent.

Moreover, recent easing of accounting standards for the US banks by the regulatory authorities further "cooked the books" for the stress tests. If all 19 large banks had been required to mark to market the value of all their assets, all 19 would now be in the market for additional tangible common equity. Whether this escape hatch was voluntarily opened up by the Treasury Secretary, or was coerced politically as a result of large bank pressures, the outcome is the same. The general public has been lured into a false sense of complacency regarding the viability of the financial sector of the economy.

Given that the four worst-performing banks now require significant additional injections of capital, and that they will be pressed into converting existing TARP preferred capital into tangible common equity, the US government will assume a significant voting presence in these (and no doubt other) banks. The impulsive and disproportional attention paid by President Obama and the Democratic Congress to the affair of the AIG bonuses early in 2009 illustrates the gulf between politicians' capacities and the needs of rational management of a financial sector.

5.10. No bail-outs for private debtors

This proposal deals directly with the problem of excessive personal indebtedness. Millions of Americans have run up debts they cannot afford, debt on credit cards, debt on auto purchases, college debt, and most significantly, debt on house purchases. There is an old joke that "If you owe the bank $1,000, you have a problem. If you owe the bank $1 million, the bank has a problem." To that, with the benefit of hindsight from September 2008, we must add: "If the bank owes $1 billion, the taxpayer has a problem."

In a political system where debtors have votes, millions of debtors are not just a problem for the debtors themselves; nor are they a problem just for the economy; they are a problem for the political system. As we have suggested earlier, limited house price reflation through monetary expansion, together with relaxed immigration laws, may be appropriate mechanisms for alleviating the public choice problem, given that the house price bubble was fueled in the first instance by excessive monetary expansion.

In the absence of constitutional guarantees (shredded by the US Supreme Court during the 1930s under pressure from FDR), will the US government support contract law when it threatens to bankrupt large numbers of politically sensitive US households? The public debate over court-enforced mortgage *"cramdowns"* signals a potential breakdown of the public-choice-compatibility of basic contract enforcement in the United States.

When private individuals and firms make bad decisions, a certain kind of discipline is provided through bankruptcy, liquidations and foreclosures. While bankruptcies involve third-party arbitration and clear violations of the original terms of private contracts, they are, under normal conditions, a key mechanism to clear out bad debts and keep the housing market functioning. Modern bankruptcy is more humane than the debtors' prisons and forced transportations favored in earlier times.

As we have seen, despite sharp declines in house prices, the US housing market still is not fully clearing. In part, the failure of markets to clear is a consequence of the financial crisis that has tightened credit. In part, however, it reflects an expectation that the government will bail out the entire market through an extensive mortgage subsidy program of the kind already initiated by the Obama administration. If such an expectation comes to pass, the government will have flashed a green light for households to re-engage in housing market speculation once the next upturn in the business cycle occurs.

We recommend that the debt crisis should be allowed to unwind without government intervention, other than through the bankruptcy courts, whenever mutually agreeable contract modifications between lender and buyer cannot be successfully concluded. By such politically costly restraint, government would clearly signal that excessive risk-taking and excessive indebtedness will be punished by market forces and that each household and each mortgage lender will be held fully responsible for its own actions.

The short-term political cost, inevitably, will be high. But such a firm policy surely will set the pattern for private, mutually beneficial contract re-negotiations between creditors and debtors; and for significant increases in personal and corporate responsibility, the only sure ways to avoid such crises from recurring with increasing intensity over time. Skeptics will surely argue that no politician will ever risk his political future to do the right thing. Public choice suggests, unfortunately, that the skeptics may prove to be correct.

6

The Regulatory Framework

The financial crisis of 2008 in the United States was primarily a failure of government: poor monetary policy, poor fiscal policy, and poor microeconomic policies. These failures have been chronicled in considerable detail in earlier chapters of this monograph. Equally important, however, was the pervasive failure of regulatory policy throughout the financial sector. Before we outline a public-choice-consistent program for regulatory reform, we must briefly review the regulatory failures that exacerbated the implosion of many major financial institutions and that threatened to freeze financial markets in the United States and elsewhere.

6.1 THE PATH TO REGULATORY FAILURE

The financial crisis began and culminated in the United States housing market. The entire episode was driven by serious political and regulatory failures, as presumably unintended consequences of poorly conceived policy institutions.

As Eamonn Butler (2009, 51) correctly notes, the roots of the housing market crisis go back to the Great Depression. At that time, credit was tight, mortgages were hard to come by, houses were not selling, and the building industry was in a state of collapse. FDR stepped in to revive the market.

A range of new institutions were created, most notably the Federal Housing Administration (FHA), which guaranteed the banks' mortgage risks, and the Federal National Mortgage Association (FNMA or Fannie Mae), which effectively insured mortgages by its willingness to purchase mortgages from lenders. In essence, these federal guarantees shifted risk from the lenders (primarily at that time the Savings & Loans institutions to the US taxpayer (Butler 2009, 52).

The Savings & Loans Institutions, unlike the banks, were not limited (by Regulation Q) as to the interest rates that they could pay their depositors. However, they were restricted to long-term mortgage business. So they borrowed short and lent long. When depositors departed without notice to secure higher interest elsewhere, the S & Ls were rendered insolvent. By 1995, their number had halved. Two other 1930s government agencies, the *Federal Savings & Loan*

Insurance Corporation (FSLC) and the *Federal Deposit Insurance Corporation* (FDIC) picked up the tab, at a cost to taxpayers of $150 billion (Butler 2009, 52). Housing market subsidies were under way with a vengeance.

Further housing market distortions were imposed by the federal government. In October 1977, President Carter had signed into law the *Community Reinvestment Act* (CRA), designed to promote home ownership for minorities. The CRA prohibited the practice of redlining, whereby banks refused mortgages in poor areas on grounds of high risk. Henceforth they must conduct business throughout the entire geographic areas that they served (Butler 2009, 53). The Carter administration had funded various community groups, such as the Association of Community Organizations for Reform Now (ACORN), to monitor performance under the CRA rules.

The mortgage lenders were already required, under the 1975 *Home Mortgage Disclosure Act* (HMDA) to provide detailed reports about whom they lent to. In 1991, HMDA rules were tightened to include a specific demand for racial equality in the institutions' lending.

In 1992, the Federal Reserve Bank of Boston published a manual advising that a mortgage applicant's lack of credit history should not be viewed negatively in a loan assessment, that borrowers should be allowed to deploy loans and gifts as deposits, and that unemployment benefits were valid income sources for lending decisions (Butler 2009, 53). The manual reminded the banks that failure to meet CRA regulations violated equal opportunity laws and exposed them to actual damages plus punitive damages of $500,000.

So the great housing bubble-party began. With credit-worthiness no longer relevant, the volume of sub-prime loans exploded. Home "ownership" in the United States increased from 65 per cent of households in 1994 to 69 per cent in 2004, representing approximately 4.6 million new homeowners. With the flow of new housing a small proportion of the total housing stock, house prices moved onto a sharp upward trend.

The government-sponsored *Fannie Mae* and *Freddie Mac*, responding to a 1992 law, pressed resources into wider home ownership objectives, eagerly endorsing high-risk sub-prime loans, and indeed securitizing bad loan packages that they offloaded world-wide (Butler 2009, 54). The FHA itself promoted the sub-prime mortgage boom by offering low-deposit loans to impoverished households. Throughout the industry, every actor recognized that the taxpayer was on the hook, should the housing market turn bad.

In these circumstances, all the major banks competed to serve the political objectives of the Bush administration. In particular, they developed "reverse redlining" programs that targeted impoverished, illiterate, officially unemployed minorities, offering low-interest, option sub-prime ARM mortgages that covered 125 per cent or more of the market valuation of the house. They sliced and diced these mortgages into securitized bonds without any concern for their underlying market values. Fannie Mae and Freddie Mac had limitless appetites for such bonds. The Office of Thrift Supervision was literally selling itself to reckless mortgage banks, offering thrift charters to anyone who would respond, on almost any terms that they cared to name.

The so-called major rating agencies had been thoroughly infiltrated by the mortgage industry and were grading junk bonds at AAA. The FDIC was half-asleep at the wheel, even after the collapse of *Indymac Bank* much earlier in 2008. The SEC had been completely comatose for at least the past eight years, even after the collapse of the dot-com bubble, and the Federal Reserve, together with the government of the People's Republic of China, had flooded the United States markets with cheap money. All of this tended to permit or encourage the bubble that burst in 2008.

6.2. A public-choice-consistent framework for regulating the financial sector

Once the current crisis has eased, political attention will predictably return to the issue of regulatory reform. Early signals suggest that the Obama administration will seek tighter regulation of the entire financial sector, socializing more risk, and creating new barriers to entry and burdens for entrepreneurship. Yet the financial world is already littered with regulatory agencies, every single one of which failed to intervene to protect the public interest over the period from 2000 to September 2008.

Richard Posner (2009, 289) identifies a partial list of such agencies that includes: the Federal Reserve, the Federal Deposit Insurance Corporation, the Securities and Exchange Commission, the Commodity Futures Trading Commission, the Federal Housing Administration, the Office of Housing Enterprise Oversight, the National Credit Union Administration, the Treasury Department and its agencies, such as the Comptroller of the Currency and the Office of Thrift Supervision, and fifty state banking and insurance commissioners. We would add to this list the government-sponsored Fannie Mae and Freddie Mac corporations and the three major credit-rating agencies, Fitch, Moody's and Standard & Poor. Fragmentation of regulatory authority provides ample opportunity for financial institutions to shop around for favorable treatment. The

2008 crisis reflects a massive failure of the conventional, broad, discretion-based, regulatory paradigm.

Two separate but reinforcing research programs, one from Chicago, the other from Virginia, provide an alternative, sounder basis for avoiding regulatory pitfalls while ensuring that capitalism does not veer off its wealth-creating tracks.

From Chicago, we learn that regulatory agencies are largely, but not completely, subservient to the institutions that they are supposed to regulate (Stigler 1971, Peltzman 1976). The regulators stretch the limits of their agency discretion to service the economic interests of their "clientele", by restricting new entry, cartelizing prices, and dampening down innovation. However, at some margin, they also reflect consumer interests as a means of maximizing their own regulatory returns. Regulators also view their regulated institutions as potential opportunities for lucrative post-regulatory employment. Once the rents created by regulation have been fully dissipated by those who are regulated, deregulation typically follows (Peltzman 1980).

From Virginia, and public choice more generally (Weingast, 1981, Weingast and Moran 1983, Rowley 1992, Rowley, Thorbecke and Wagner 1995), we learn that US federal regulatory agencies respond systematically to signals from their House and Senate oversight and appropriations committees/sub-committees, and from the executive branch of government. They are indeed creatures of the current political system. Where the goals of the polity differ from the original intent of the legislation, regulatory agencies follow their current masters, not the past initiators, unless their statutory remits are tightly drawn.

The lessons learned from Chicago with those learned from Virginia can be combined into an account of why regulation failed to prevent the financial crisis of 2008. The political system was fueled by campaign funding from myopic financial institutions, while it adored reverse-redlining policies as "do-good" politics. The financial institutions were apparently awash with profits from the securitized mortgage markets. Consumers were lulled into a false sense of security as house prices soared, as 401 (k) portfolios boomed, and as access to cheap credit fueled durable consumption good purchases. No one had any apparent cause for personal concern. And, predictably, no one cared at all about the long-term public interest.

In proposing a new regulatory framework for the US financial sector, we start with the assumption that limited liability, despite all its weaknesses, is here to stay. We also assume that FDIC protection is here to stay. Given these assumptions, a great deal of moral hazard is already built into the financial sector. The trick is to avoid introducing additional moral hazard via regulatory policy.

First, it should be a rule of governance for the financial sector that the federal government will never again provide bail-out loans or gifts (subsidies) to the financial sector. "Every tub must stand on its own bottom" must be the presumption for any well motivated capitalist system. The second rule of governance is that any insolvent financial institution will be forced into bankruptcy, either to reorganize or to liquidate its assets. Shareholders and bondholders of such institutions should know that their investments are completely at risk at all times. No organization should ever be viewed as "too big to fail."

Second, there should be a restoration of some kind of separation between commercial banking functions, which will be eligible for FDIC protection, and investment banking operations, which will be permitted only to institutions whose potential losses will be borne solely by their own shareholders and bondholders. This objective could be achieved by re-enactment of the relevant sections of the *Glass-Steagall Act* of 1933.

Commercial banking, narrowly defined to include only the clearing banks that take deposits and engage in check-clearing and payment settlements, should be restored to its primary roots as a store of value and a facilitator of exchange, lending primarily to well known customers, both households and firms, tightly controlled by the FDIC with the goal of protecting deposits. FDIC protection should be extended only to banks that strictly satisfy these functional requirements. Any FDIC-insured bank that deviates from these functions should lose its FDIC protection. Only FDIC-insured banks should have access to the lender-of-last resort facility of the Federal Reserve.

Even with respect to FDIC-insured commercial banks, the threat of failure must remain. Their shareholders and their bondholders must expect to lose their investments should the bank fail. FDIC rules regarding minimum cash reserve to total asset ratios and minimum tangible common equity (TCE) to total asset ratios would strictly apply. Despite their documented weaknesses (Myddleton 2009, 103-4), mark to market accounting rules should be applied for FDIC purposes. Banks that fail to maintain the two ratios should be moved into bankruptcy by the FDIC. Regulatory discretion should be minimized.

FDIC should require bi-annual financial statements from every FDIC-insured bank, outlining financial ratios and describing by category and, where relevant, by credit-agency rating, all loans and investments that have been made. This information should be provided by the banks to all its depositors, as well as to its shareholders and bondholders. Information transparency (Beenstock

2009, 59-60) would then become a central feature of the commercial banking sector.

To ensure that the FDIC is able to meet its insurance commitments without recourse to taxpayer bail-outs, FDIC rates should be increased on all commercial banks to ensure that its reserves cover at least 5 per cent (raised from the current 2 per cent) of all insured deposits. The FDIC should impose a first charge deductible on the shareholders of any bank that fails to protect its depositors against a bank run.

Only the clearing banks should receive FDIC protection. To retain such protection, the clearing banks should be required to divest themselves of investment banking ancillaries. The rationale for this is straight forward. Conglomerate banks presently contain large hedge funds, assemblies of speculative trading positions. If a hedge fund loses say 5 per cent of its assets, and investors seek to liquidate their positions, the hedge fund can suspend redemptions. But if a clearing bank loses 5 per cent of its assets, it is bust (Kay 2009, 178-9). That is why segmentation of the two functions is essential.

It has been suggested that all financial institutions should be subjected to the same regulations as those that enjoy FDIC protection. We reject this view. As long as there is adequate transparency, and all potential shareholders, creditors and counterparties are forewarned that no bail-out will ever be countenanced, a competitive United States market in investment banking will self-regulate and will be more innovative than under regulation. *Caveat emptor* is the appropriate rule of conduct for any individual who buys the stocks and bonds of investment banks. This *laissez-faire* policy will help the United States to retain its role as the leading international financial center. It is no accident that New York and London, rather than the more heavily regulated Paris and Frankfurt, were viewed as world-class financial centers until September 2008.

Strict, conservative rules should govern lending and borrowing in the house mortgage industry, to the extent that the operations of this industry impose potential liabilities on the taxpayer through the FDIC. For example, FDIC-insured banks should be prohibited from making any home mortgage loan that exceeds 90 per cent of the market value of a property, with borrowers making deposits of at least 10 per cent of the market value of the property. Rules might prohibit mortgage balloon payments, and any ARM of shorter duration than 5 years, or even require borrowers to furnish copies of their latest 1040 income tax returns when applying for a loan, to prove that mortgage repayment schedules do not exceed 30 per cent of the annual gross adjusted income of a household. These restrictions of freedom of contract are justified by the need to ensure that banks which enjoy FDIC insurance do not play a game of "heads we win, tails the taxpayer loses."

Non-FDIC-insured institutions may engage in any mortgage practices consistent with the common law, but the Securities and Exchange Commission should ensure that their practices are fully disclosed to the shareholders and bondholders who will be the sole losers in the event of a failure of these institutions.

Finally, we evaluate the role played by the three major credit ratings agencies in the United States 2008 financial crisis (Morrison 2009). Clearly, many structured financial products were far less safe than they appeared to be from the creditworthiness assessments of the major ratings agencies. Many highest rated bonds (assigned an Aaa or AAA by the agencies) turned out to be of C (or junk bond) status. Even sophisticated investors were misled by these ratings errors. Market prices clearly move in response to changes in credit ratings, indicating a perhaps excessive reliance upon ratings by market investors.

Why did the rating system fail so dramatically and what, if anything should be done to prevent a recurrence of this failure? Credit ratings agencies sell opinions, much in the same way as newspapers. There are few advocates for regulating newspapers, as long as they avoid such legal pitfalls as libel. Similarly, the case for regulating credit ratings agencies is weak. The best safeguard against incompetence or prejudice is free entry and high transparency, especially in view of changes since 1970 in the way that credit ratings are paid for.

Prior to 1970, credit ratings were paid for by investors, essentially enabling small investors to free-ride on ratings paid for by larger investors. Market failure resulted, making it uneconomic to rate some issues (Morrison 2009, 123). In consequence, issuers began to pay for their own ratings. The potential for corruption this practice creates is self-evident. One solution, that we advocate, is that the credit ratings agencies be required to attach a warning label to any credit rating associated with the product of an institution that has paid for that rating, with the Securities and Exchange Commission acting as third party enforcer for the completeness and accuracy of such disclosures.

A second problem arises as a result of regulation itself. In the United States, bank capital regulations rely on ratings. When investment choices are restricted by ratings, agencies serve as gatekeepers: "They sell admission to the regulated investment management and banking markets" (Morrison 2009, 125). The rating agency's rational action is to charge high fees to assist issuers in their search for strong ratings. A regulated market with restricted entry lowers the concern for accuracy.

Further deregulation would prevent ratings agencies from profiting from regulatory anomalies. Allow free entry into the credit ratings industry, and allow financial institutions (other than commercial banks) full freedom to select their own portfolios. In a full-information situation, a competitive credit ratings industry will pursue honest ratings for reputational reasons (Becker 1957).

Such a combination of strict, transparent, non-discretionary rules will provide a level playing field across the financial sector and will surely prevent any repetition of the 2008 financial crisis. It will do so within a regulatory framework that supports *laissez-faire* capitalism.

7

Conclusions

The United States economy is rich both in physical and in human capital. Within itself, it contains powerful restorative impulses capable of moving through the trough of contraction into the next upturn of the business cycle. In late 2008, the key obstacles to such restoration were the financial crisis, the massive private and public debt overhang, and pessimistic expectations. Since then, a wave of government interventions has introduced new obstacles that may prove even more debilitating: political risk, and incentives for rent-seeking. Unfortunately, plans seem to be underway to introduce still more policies that impede market recovery.

Now is a particularly bad time to enact socialistic reforms to the market for healthcare, pursue wealth-destructive cap and trade environmental programs, or force additional federal tax dollars into state and local education markets. Such policies imply higher government spending and, eventually, either higher taxes or runaway inflation, thus depleting taxpayer and business confidence in the economy and driving a further collapse in stock market value.

It is not too difficult to explain the stylized facts of the past decade in terms of basic economic intuitions, such as scarcity, and that people respond to incentives. In the late 1990s, government spending was restrained, and the economy boomed. In the 2000s, government spending started rising and, since resources are scarce, private investment fell. With less private investment, economic growth became less robust and created fewer jobs. Easy money from the Federal Reserve, and capital inflows from abroad, buoyed the economy temporarily, fueling a surge in debt and a housing price bubble in the process.

When house prices started to fall, mortgage debt went bad, bringing down the financial industry with it. The burden of government grew, and the economy paid the price. What is the solution? Shrink the government back to the size it was in the 1990s. Yet this simple supply-side logic is being drowned out by old-fashioned Keynesian demand-side stories that are scantily supported empirically and theoretically flawed.

The policies we recommend (except to some extent on immigration) are so opposed to anything that can realistically be expected from a government that was elected with the help of the campaign contributions of organized labor, organized environmental groups, organized healthcare workers, organized teachers unions, organized farmers and poorly-performing businesses seeking government contracts, that it may seem as quixotic to advocate them now as it was for Adam Smith (1776) to attack the mercantilism that was the reigning misguided philosophy of the late eighteenth century.

His comment (Smith 1782) that "There is a great deal of ruin in a nation" captures his despairing awareness of the barriers his advocacy faced. Yet Smith clung to reason, and, in the next few decades, his arguments transformed economic policy in Britain. In the same way, we stand by reason, hoping that the American people, and possibly even American political leaders, eventually will see the light.

As Adam Smith might well have put it, had he thought it even remotely possible for governments to grow to levels now common in the early twenty-first century: *capitalism succeeds and big government fails to raise the wealth of nations.* As formerly free market scholars such as Richard Posner (2009) peel away from this judgment and run for the cover provided by big government, *Remnants*[7] such as we must ensure that the small candle of liberty continues to shine on through the new Dark Age that threatens.

Like Adam Smith in 1776, we conclude this monograph on a note of tentative optimism for the future of *laissez-faire* capitalism in the United States. In our judgment, the current recession is by no means as deep as President Obama and his administration would have us believe. By exaggerating the seriousness of the economic contraction, the President has opened up avenues for a full-blooded pursuit of a much more far-ranging, left-leaning economic agenda than the majority of Americans would normally endorse.

By so doing, he may well have overreached, just as President Lyndon Johnson overreached with his pursuit of war escalation in Vietnam and the *Great Society* Program following his defeat of Senator Barry Goldwater in 1964. Liberal overreach in the Great Society era ended the great post-Second World War boom and caused over a decade of slowdown and stagnation, but eventually paved the way for a generation of conservative dominance and strong economic growth after the election of Ronald Reagan in 1980.

In normal times, a majority of Americans prefers *laissez-faire* capitalism to the social market economy. The US economy is dynamic because a large ma-

---

[7] This is a term introduced by Lawrence Read to identify those thinkers and scholars who stand aside from transient pressures and carry the eternal message of liberty across the ages.

jority of Americans like it that way. Even in times of boom, 15 per cent of American jobs disappear each year. Their places are taken by new jobs created by start-ups and expansions.

This dynamism continues even in the midst of the 2008-9 financial collapse. As Starbucks and Neiman Marcus encounter problems, companies that cater to a more frugal clientele, Burger King and Wal-Mart, expand and prosper. That is the American way. A Pew poll released on May 21, 2009 found that 76 per cent of Americans still agree that the country's strength is "mostly based on the success of American business" and 90 per cent still admire people who "get rich by working hard" (*The Economist*, May 30, 2009, 13).

As the consequences of the Obama government's profligate deficit-spending and interventionism become clear, and US voters face rising taxes, high interest rates, and continuing below-trend economic growth, disillusionment inevitably will set in, and may express itself politically as a reformed Republican Party revival, or as a shift to the right by a reforming Democratic Party, as occurred to some extent in the 1990s.

Western European economies, especially the bastion of state-dominated capitalism, France, should serve as a cautionary tale of what awaits America in the long run if such an awakening fails to occur. In France, the average rate of unemployment rarely falls below 8 per cent, even at the peak of the business cycle; and the average youth unemployment rate almost always exceeds 20 per cent. In France, more than 20 per cent of all available jobs are provided through government, and many of these are relatively poorly paid make-work, in the form of cleaning the facades of public buildings, planting and weeding public gardens and the like. In France, more than 50 per cent of GDP is accounted for by public spending. The rate of GDP growth in France lags permanently below the average for OECD countries. (*The Economist*, May 9, 2009, 27-29).

The United States has enjoyed much greater success in the past quarter of a century because its system is far more *laissez-faire*, and can anticipate similar success in the future if the recent drift to state dominance is reversed. We anticipate that a return to the kind of *laissez-faire* capitalism that evolved so successfully throughout the last two decades of the twentieth century once again will enjoy majority support in the not-too-far-distant future once the electorate begins to suffer the severe economic downside of the Bush and the Obama administrations' anti-capitalist policies.

Bibliography

"A 40-Year-Old Wish List," (2009). *Wall Street Journal*, January 28. Yahoo!Finance. http://finance.yahoo.com/

Alchian, A.A. and Demsetz, H. (1972). "Production, Information Costs, and Economic Organization". *American Economic Review* 62, 777-95.

Bagehot, W. (1873/1978). "Lombard Street", in N. St. John Stevas (ed.), *The Collected Works of Walter Bagehot*, Vol. IX, London: The Economist, 78, 132.

Bagus, P. and Schiml, M.H. (2009). "The Insolvency of the Fed". *Mises Daily*, February 5.

Bank of International Settlements (2008). *78th Annaul Report*. Basel: Switzerland.

Barro, R.J. (1974). "Are Government Bonds Net Wealth?" *Journal of Political Economy*, 84 (6), 1095-117.

Becker, G.S. (1957). *The Economics of Discrimination*. Chicago: University of Chicago Press.

Becker, G.S. (1983). "A Theory of Competition Among Pressure Groups for Political Influence". *Quarterly Journal of Economics*, 63, 371-400.

Becker, G.S. and Murphy, K.M. (2009). "There's No Stimulus Free Lunch". *Wall Street Journal*, February 10.

Beenstock, M. (2009). "Market foundations for the new financial architecture" in *Verdict on the Crash: Causes and Policy Implications*, edited by P. Booth. London: Institute of Economic Affairs, 59-72.

Bernanke, B.S. (1983). "Non-Monetary Effects of the Financial Crisis in the Propagation of the Great Depression". *American Economic Review*, 73 (3), 257-276.

Bernanke, B.S. (2000). *Essays on the Great Depression*. Princeton: Princeton University Press.

Bernanke, B.S. (2009). "Four Questions about the Financial Crisis". http://www.federalreserve.gov/newsevents/speech/bernanke20090414a.htm

Booth, P. (2009) (ed.) *Verdict on the Crash: Causes and Policy Implications*. London: Institute of Economic Affairs.

Booth, P. (2009). "Introduction" in *Verdict on the Crash: Causes and Policy Implications*, edited by P. Booth. London: Institute of Economic Affairs, 27-33.

Booth, P. (2009). "More regulation, less regulation or better regulation?" in *Verdict on the Crash: Causes and Policy Implications* edited by P. Booth. London: Institute of Economic Affairs, 157-170.

Brooks, D. "Taking Depression Seriously." (2009). *New York Times*, March 9.

Brennan, H.G. and Buchanan, J.M. (1980). "The Logic of the Ricardian Equivalence Theorem". *Finanzarchiv*, 38 (1), 4-16.

Brunnermeier, M.K. (2009). "Deciphering the Liquidity and Credit Crunch 2007-2008". *Journal of Economic Perspectives*, 23 (1), 77-100.

Buchanan, J.M. (1958). "Concerning Future Generations", in Chapter Four, and "A Suggested Conceptual Revaluation of the National Debt", Appendix, in J.M. Buchanan, *Public Principles of Public Debt: A Defense and Restatement*. Homewood, IL: Richard D. Irwin, Inc., 31-47 and 196-215.

Buchanan, J.M. (1964). "Public Debt, Cost Theory, and the Fiscal Illusion", in J.M. Ferguson (ed.), *Public Debt and Future Generations*. Chapel Hill, NC: University of North Carolina Press, 150-63.

Buchanan, J.M. (1966). "The Icons of Public Debt". *Journal of Finance*, XXI, 544-6.

Buchanan, J.M. (1969). *Cost and Choice*. Chicago: Markham Publishing Company.

Buchanan, J.M. and Tullock, G. (1962). *The Calculus of Consent.* Ann Arbor: University of Michigan Press.

Buchanan, J.M. and Wagner, R.E. (1977) *Democracy in Deficit: The Political Legacy of Lord Keynes.* New York: Academic Press.

Buchanan, J.M., Rowley, C.K. and Tollison, R.D. (eds.), (1986). *Deficits.* Oxford: Basil Blackwell.

Buiter, W. (2009). "Good Bank/New Bank vs. Bad Bank: a rare example of a no-brainer". *Financial Times*, February 8.

Bush, G.W. (2004). "Speech to Republican National Convention". http://www.cbsnews.com/stories/2004/09/02/politics/main640596.shtml

Butler, E. (2009). "The financial crisis: blame governments, not bankers" in *Verdict on the Crash: Causes and Policy Implications*, edited by P. Booth. London: Institute of Economic Affairs, 51-58.

Cecchetti, S.G. (2009). "Crisis and Responses: The Federal Reserve in the Early Stages of the Financial Crisis". *Journal of Economic Perspectives*, 23, (1), 51-76.

Chantrill, C. (2009). "The Great Depression: Facts, Charts, History, Analysis, Opinion". http://www.usstuckonstupid.com/sos.html

Cole, H.L and Ohanian, L.E. (2001). "New Deal policies and the persistence of the Great Depression: a general equilibrium analysis", *Working Paper* 597. Federal Reserve Bank of Minneapolis.

Congdon, T. (2009). *Central Banking in a Free Society.* London: Institute of Economic Affairs.

Congleton, R.D. (2009). "On the Political Economy of the Financial Crisis and Bailout of 2008". Fairfax: Center for Study of Public Choice Working Paper.

Couch, J.F. and Shughart, W.F. II. (1998). *The Political Economy of the New Deal.* Cheltenham, UK and Northampton, USA: Edward Elgar Publishing.

Couch, J.F. and Shughart, W.F. II. (2000). "New Deal spending and the states: the politics of public works", in J.C. Heckleman, J.C. Moorhouse and R.M. Whaples (eds.) *Public Choice Interpretations of American Economic History.* Boston: Kluwer Academic Publishers, 105-122.

Coval, J., Jurek, J., and Stafford, E. (2009). "The Economics of Structured Finance". *Journal of Economic Perspectives,* 23, (1), 3-26.

De Long, J.B. and Summers, L.H. (1986). "How Does Macroeconomic Policy Affect Output?" *American Economic Review,* 76, (December), 1031-1044.

"Did Quantitative easing by the Bank of Japan Work?" http://www.frbsf.org/publications/economics/letter/2006/el2006-28.html

Dowd, K. (2009). "Moral Hazard and the Financial Crisis". *The Cato Journal,* 29 (1), 141-166.

Downs, A. (1957). *An Economic Theory of Democracy.* New York: Harper and Row.

Eichengreen, B. (1992). *Golden Fetters: The Gold Standard and the Great Depression 1919-1939.* New York: Oxford University Press.

Evans, M. and Wachtel, P. (1993). "Were Price Changes During the Great Depression Anticipated? Evidence From Nominal Interest Rates". *Journal of Monetary Economics* 32 (1), 193-220.

Fackler, J.S. and Parker, R.E. (2001). "Was Debt Deflation Operative During the Great Depression?" East Carolina University Working Paper.

Fama, E. (1980). "Agency Problems and the Theory of the Firm". *Journal of Political Economy* 88, 288-307.

Fisher, I. (1911). *The Purchasing Power of Money.* New York: Macmillan.

Bibliography

Fisher, I. (1920). *Stabilizing the Dollar.* New York: Macmillan.

Fisher, I. (1933). "The Debt Deflation Theory of Great Depressions". *Econometrica*, I, (4), 337-57.

Fleming, J.M. (1962). "Domestic Financial Policies under Fixed and under Floating Exchange Rates". *IMF Staff Papers,* 9 (November), 369-379.

Friedman, M. (1956) *Studies in the Quantity Theory of Money.* Chicago: University of Chicago Press.

Friedman, M. (1957). *A Theory of the Consumption Function.* Princeton: Princeton University Press.

Friedman, M. (1962). *Capitalism and Freedom.* Chicago: University of Chicago Press.

Friedman, M. (1968). "The role of monetary policy". *American Economic Review*, 58 (March), 1-17.

Friedman, M. and Schwartz, A.J. (1963). *A Monetary History of the United States, 1867-1960.* Princeton: Princeton University Press.

Galbraith, J.K. (1958). *The Affluent Society.* New York: Houghton Mifflin.

Goodhart, C.A.E. (2009). *The Regulatory Response to the Financial Crisis.* Aldershot and Northampton: Edward Elgar Publishing.

Gordon, J.S. (2004). *An Empire of Wealth: The Epic History of American Economic Power.* New York: HarperCollins.

Gordon, R.J. (1974). *Milton Friedman's Monetary Framework: A Debate With His Critics.* Chicago: University of Chicago Press.

"Gramm-Leach-Bliley Act" (1999). http://en.wikipedia.org/wiki/Gramm-Leach-Bliley Act

Greenlees, J. and McClelland, R. (2008). "Common Misconceptions about the Consumer Price Index: Questions and Answers". http://www.bls.gov/cpi/cpiqa.html

Grynbaum, M.M. (2008). "Study Finds Flawed Practices at Ratings Firms". http://www.nytimes.com/2008/07/09/business/09credit.html

Hamilton, J.D. (1987). "Monetary Factors in the Great Depression". *Journal of Monetary Economics* 13, 1-25.

Hayek, F.A. (1933/1975). *Monetary Theory and the Trade Cycle*. New York: Augustus Kelley.

Hayek, F.A. (1935/67). *Prices and Production*. New York: Augustus Kelley.

Hayek, F.A. (1944). *The Road to Serfdom*. Chicago: University of Chicago Press.

Hayek, F.A. (1960). *The Constitution of Liberty*. London: Routledge & Kegan Paul.

Higgs, R. (1987). *Crisis and Leviathan: Critical Episodes in the Growth of American Government*. New York and Oxford: Oxford University Press.

Hodges, M.W. (2007). "America's Total Debt Report http://mwhodges.home.att.net/nat-debt-a.html.

Hoover Institution. (2009). "Facts on Policy: Consumer Debt". http://www.hoover.org/research/factsonpolicy/facts/38837147.html

Hulse, C. and Herszenhorn, D.M. (2009). "House Approves 90% Tax on Bonuses After Bailouts". *The New York Times*, March 20.

Issing, O. (2009). "Asset Prices and Monetary Policy". *The Cato Journal,* 29 (1), 45-52.

Kay, J. (2009). "The future of financial services regulation", in *Verdict on the Crash: Causes and Policy Implications*, edited by P. Booth. London: Institute of Economic Affairs, 177-182.

Bibliography

Keynes, J.M. (1936). *The General Theory of Employment, Interest, and Money*. London: Macmillan.

Kindleberger, C.P. (1973). *The World in Depression*, 1929-1939. Berkeley: University of California Press.

Knight, F. (undated/1991). "The Case for Communism: From the Standpoint of an Ex-Liberal". Published posthumously in *Research in the History of Economic Thought and Methodology*, edited by Warren J. Samuels, archival supplement 2 , 57-108.

Kohn, D.L. (2009). "Monetary Policy and Asset Prices Revisited". *The Cato Journal*, 29 (1), 31-44.

Krugman, P. (2009). "Banking on the Brink". *The New York Times*, February 22.

Lanman, S. (2009). "Rambo Fed' Will Buy Treasuries to Combat Crisis." *Bloomberg*, March19,2009. http://www.bloomberg.com/apps/news?pid=20601087&sid=a1eJEhHYb0yA&refer=home

Lerner, A.P. (1943). "Functional Finance and the Federal Debt". *Social Research*, 10 (1), 38-51.

Lerner, A.P. (1948). "The Burden of the National Debt". in *Income, Employment and Public Policy: Essays in Honor of Alvin Hansen*. New York: W.W. Norton and Company, 255-75.

Lindmark, T. (2009). "Obama's Auto Task Force Lacks Expertise". http://seekingalpha.com/article/120861-obama-s-auto-task-force-lacks-expertise

Lucas, R.E. (1972). "Expectations and the Neutrality of Money". *Journal of Economic Theory*, 4 (April), 103-24.

Lucas, R.E. (1975). "An Equilibrium Model of the Business Cycle". *Journal of Political Economy*, 83 (December), 1113-1144.

Lucas, R.E. (1976). "Econometric Policy Evaluation: A Critique". *Carnegie-Rochester Conference Series on Public Policy*, 1, 19-46.

Mayer, C., Pence, K., and Sherlunde, S.M. (2009). "The Rise in Mortgage Defaults". *Journal of Economic Perspectives*, 23 (1), 27-50.

Melloan, G. (2009). "Why 'Stimulus' Will Mean Inflation". *The Wall Street Journal*, February 6.

Meltzer, A.H. (2009). "Reflections on the Financial Crisis". *The Cato Journal*, 29 (1), 25-30.

Miron, J.A. (2009). "Bailout or Bankruptcy". *The Cato Journal* 29, (1), 1-17.

Mises, L. von. (1912/1981). *The Theory of Money and Credit*. Indianapolis: Liberty Classics.

"Monetizing the Debt: Fed Will Buy Everything That's Not Nailed Down." March 19, 2009. http://prudentinvestor.blogspot.com/2009/o3/monetizing-debt-fed-will-buy-everything.html

Morrison, A.D. (2009). "Ratings agencies, regulation and financial market stability" in *Verdict on the Crash: Causes and Policy Implications*, edited by P. Booth. London: Institute of Economic Affairs, 117-128.

Mundell, R.A. (1968). *International Economics*. New York: Macmillan.

Myddleton, D.R. (2009). "Accounting aspects of the financial crisis", in *Verdict on the crash: Causes and Policy Implications*, edited by P. Booth. London: Institute of Economic Affairs, 101-108.

Niskanen, W. A. (1971). *Bureaucracy and Representative Government*. New York: Aldine-Atherton.

O'Driscoll, G.P. (2009). "Money and the Present Crisis". *The Cato Journal*, 29 (1), 167-186.

Olson, M. (1965). *The Logic of Collective Action*. Cambridge: Harvard University Press.

Parker, R. (2009). "Án Overview of the Great Depression". http://eh.net/encyclopedia/article/parker/depression

Peltzman, S. (1976). "Toward a More General Theory of Regulation". *Journal of Law and Economics*, XIX, (2), 211-40.

Poole, W. (2009). "The Way Forward: Incentives, Not Regulations". *The Cato Journal,* 29 (1), 201-208.

Posner, R.A. (2009). A Failure of Capitalism: *The Crisis of '08 and the Descent Into Depression*. Cambridge, Mass. and London, England: Harvard University Press.

Posner R.A. (2009a). "Is the Stock Market Efficient?" http://www.becker-posner-blog.com (accessed on April 13, 2009).

Powell, J. (2003). *FDR's Folly: How Roosevelt and His New Deal Prolonged the Great Depression*. New York: Crown Forum.

Rand, A. (1957). *Atlas Shrugged*. New York: Random House.

Reed, L.W. (1981/2008). *Great Myths of the Great Depression*. Midland, Michigan: Mackinac Center for Public Policy.

Reynolds, M. (2009). "How the Obama plan will affect homeowners". *Los Angeles Times*, February 19

Ricardo, D. (1821/1951). "Taxes on Other Commodities than Raw Produce" in P. Sraffa (ed.) with M.H. Dobb, *The Works and Correspondence of David Ricardo, Volume 1: On the Principles of Political Economy and Taxation*, Chapter XVII. Cambridge: Cambridge University Press, 243-56.

Romer, C.D. (1990). "The Great Crash and the Onset of the Great Depression". *Quarterly Journal of Economics*, 105 (3), 597-624.

Romer, C.D. (1992). "What Ended the Great Depression?" *Journal of Economic History*, 52 (4), 757-84.

Romer, C.D. (1993). 'The Nation in Depression'. *Journal of Economic Perspectives*, 7, 19-39.

Romer, D. (2006). *Advanced Macroeconomics*. New York: McGraw-Hill.

Romer, P. (2009). "Let's Start Brand New Banks: A clean slate would keep TARP away from bad banks". *The Wall Street Journal*, February 6.

Rothbard, M. (1962). *Man, Economy and the State: A Treatise on Economic Principles*. Princeton, NJ: D. Van Nostrand Co.

Rowley, C.K. (1993). *Liberty and the State*. Aldershot and Brookfield: Edward Elgar Publishing.

Rowley, C.K. (2004). "Public Choice and Constitutional Political Economy", in C.K. Rowley and F. Schneider (eds.) *The Encyclopedia of Public Choice*, Volume I. Dordrecht, Boston and London: Kluwer Academic Publishers.

Rowley, C.K. (2005). "Fragmenting parchment and the winds of war". *Public Choice*, 124, (1-2), 33-56.

Rowley, C.K., Thorbecke, W. and Wagner, R.E. (1995). *Trade Protection in the United States*. Aldershot, UK and Brookfield, USA: Edward Elgar Publishing.

Rowley, C.K. and Vachris, M.A. (1996). "The Virginia School of Political Economy" in F. Foldvary (ed.) *Beyond Neoclassical Economics: Heterodox Approaches to Economic Theory*. Aldershot: Edward Elgar Publishing, 61-82.

Rowley, C.K., Shughart, W.F., II, and Tollison, R.D. (eds.) (2004). *The Economics of Budget Deficits*, Volumes I and II.: Cheltenham, UK and Northampton, USA: Edward Elgar Publishing.

Samuelson, P.A. (1948). "Fiscal Policy and Full Employment Without Inflation", in P.A. Samuelson, *Economics: An Introductory Analysis*, First Edition, New York: McGraw-Hill Book Company, Inc., 409-43

Bibliography

Samuelson, P.A. and Solow, R.M. (1960). "Analytical Aspects of Anti-Inflation Policy". *American Economic Review*, 50 (May), 177-194.

Samwick, A.A. (2009). "Moral Hazard in the Policy response to the 2008 Financial Market Meltdown". *The Cato Journal*, 29 (1), 131-140.

Schlesinger, A. (1958). *The Coming of the New Deal*. Boston: Houghton Mifflin.

Schumpeter, J. A. (1942). *Capitalism, Socialism and Democracy*. New York: Harper and Row.

Schwartz, A.J. (2009). "Origins of the Financial Market Crisis of 2008". *The Cato Journal* 29 (1), 19-24.

Shughart, W.F. II. (2004). "New Deal", in C.K. Rowley and F. Schneider (eds.) *The Encyclopedia of Public Choice*. Volume II. Dordrecht, Boston and London: Kluwer Academic Publishers, 394-397.

Shughart, W. F. II. (2004). "Regulation and Antitrust", in C.K. Rowley and F. Schneider (eds.) *The Encyclopedia of Public Choice*. Volume I. Dordrecht, Boston, and London: Kluwer Academic Publishers, 263-283.

Smith, A. (1776/1976). "Of Publick Debts", in R.H. Campbell, A.S. Skinner and W.B. Todd (eds.). *An Inquiry into the Nature and Causes of the Wealth of Nations*, Volume II, Book V, Chapter III. Oxford: Clarendon Press, 907-47.

Smith, A. (1782). Letter 221, addressed to Sir John Sinclair, dated 14, October, 1782.

Solow, R.M. (2009). "How to Understand the Disaster". *The New York Review of Books*, 56 (8), May 14.

Stigler, G.J. (1971). "The Theory of Economic Regulation". *Bell Journal of Economics and Management Science*, 2, 137-46.

Summers.L. (1988). "Relative Wages, Efficiency Wages, and Keynesian Unemployment". *American Economic Review*, 78 (3), 383-388.

Taylor, J.B. (2009) Getting Off Track. Stanford: Hoover Institution Press.

The Economist (2009). "Wild-animal spirits: Why is finance so unstable? January 24-30, 6-22.

The Economist (2009). "Briefing Irving Fisher: Out of Keynes's shadow". February 14-20, 78-79.

The Economist (2009). "Dashed expectations: Tim Geithner hopes to restore stability to the banking system by luring private investors. The devil will be in the missing detail". February 14-20, 83-4.

The Economist (2009). "A ghoulish prospect: Nationalization carries risks, but it may still be the best way to deal with American bankings' undead". February 28-March 5, 73-75.

The Economist (2009). "Economics Focus: Cycle-proof regulation". April 11-17, 79.

The Economist (2009). "Barack Obama and the carmakers: an offer you can't refuse". May 9-15, 14.

The Economist (2009). "Vive la difference". May 9-15, 27-29.

The Economist (2009). "Deflation in America: The greater of two evils". May 9-15, 16-18.

The Economist (2009). "Piling on: In his zeal to fix capitalism, Barack Obama must not stifle America's dynamism." May 30.

Tollison, R.D. (2004). "Public Choice From The Perspective of Economics", in C.K. Rowley and F. Schneider (eds.) The Encyclopedia of Public Choice. Volume I. Dordrecht, Boston and London: Kluwer Academic Publishers, 191-201.

Tullock, G. (1967). "The Welfare Costs of Tariffs, Monopolies and Theft". Western Economic Journal, 5, 224-32.

Tullock, G. (1980. "Efficient Rent Seeking", in J.M. Buchanan, R.D. Tollison and G. Tullock (eds.), *Towards a Theory of the Rent-Seeking Society*. College Station: Texas A. & M. University Press.

Wanniski, J. (1978). "Taxes, Revenues and the 'Laffer Curve'". *Public Interest*.

Weingast, B.R. (1995). "The economic role of political institutions: market-preserving federalism and economic development". *Journal of Law, Economics and Organization*, Vol. 11, No. 1, 1-31.

White, L.H. (2009). "Federal Reserve Policy and the Housing Bubble". *The Cato Journal*, 29 (1), 115-26.

Wood, G. (2009). "Thoughtful regulation" in *Verdict on the Crash: Causes and Policy Implications*, edited by P. Booth. London: Institute of Economic Affairs, 171-176.

Court Cases

Carter v. Carter Coal Co., 298 U.S. 238, 56 S. Ct. 855 (1936).

Lochner v. New York, 198 U.S. 45, 25 S. Ct. 539 (1905).

Morehead v. New York ex rel. Tipaldo, 298 U.S. 587, 56 S. Ct. 918 (1936).

Schechter Poultry Corp. v. United States, 295 U.S. 495, 55 S. Ct. 837 (1935).

West Coast Hotel v. Parrish et ux, 300 U.S. 379, 57 S. Ct. 578 (1937).

Author Index

Afterword

Richard E. Wagner

W hen James Buchanan and I published *Democracy in Deficit* in 1977, we thought we were doing little more than sketching some obvious points about the political legacy of Keynesian-style economics. Prior to the Keynesian revolution, governments pretty much followed an old-style fiscal religion where they borrowed to help finance wars and depressions but ran budget surpluses during normal times to reduce their debt. According to this old-style fiscal religion, governments were subject to the same principles of prudent conduct as were individuals. Adam Smith expressed this point cogently in 1776 when he asserted that "What is prudence in the conduct of every private family can scarce be folly in that of a great kingdom."

The Keynesian revolution inverted that old-time fiscal religion. It argued that what is folly in the conduct of a private family can be prudence for a government. It is folly for individuals to borrow to finance their ordinary activities. For governments, however, those prudential limits on deficit spending don't apply, according to the Keynesian inversion of Adam Smith. The Keynesian revolution, we should remember arose in the midst of a widespread belief among Western intellectuals in the superiority of collectivist systems of economic planning. Paul Samuelson was extolling the virtues of the Soviet system in his widely adopted *Economics* text, and continued to do so even after the collapse of the Soviet Union. In contrast, Warren Nutter was widely pilloried by economists and other intellectuals for his 1962 analysis in *The Growth of Industrial Production in the Soviet Union* that Soviet communism was anemic in comparison to Western-style capitalism, and would continue to be so provided only that the West did not succumb to such collectivist nostrums.

The intellectual climate of opinion, however, was all too ready to embrace the Keynesian vision of the use of fiscal activism to override what free markets would allow. The Keynesian revolution envisioned a governmental Prometheus that had broken the chains of the old-time religion: ordinary mortals would be bound by that religion, but not governments. Where individuals had to be concerned about excessive debt, governments did not. To be sure, a sober economist could argue that the Keynesian revolution did not truly invert the old-time religion, but only changed how it would be practiced. Governments, however, are not run by sober economists. They are run by politicians, and this makes all the difference.

Democracy in Deficit was not about the economics of Keynes; it was about the political implications of the infusion of the Keynesian orientation into political practice. Prior to Keynes, normal expectations held that prudent government conduct required budget surpluses in normal times in order to provide for the periodic crises represented by wars and depressions. The Keynesian revolution operated on this climate of opinion by changing beliefs about what constituted prudent fiscal conduct. Most significantly, the absence of surpluses during normal times no longer was regarded as a sign of fiscal irresponsibility. Hence, governments would operate under a fiscal asymmetry wherein budget surpluses would be accidental events that would be quickly dissipated through new spending, while budget deficits became a normal mode of fiscal conduct.

The Keynesian-inspired change in the climate of opinion might have been innocuous could it have been confined to the classroom blackboards. But it entered into democratic politics, where it had a particularly corrosive effect. It is in the nature of politicians to want to spend money in support of programs they favor. They wouldn't run for office if they didn't want to do such things. Under the old-time fiscal religion, politicians could support new spending programs only to the extent they were willing to impose new taxes, because in normal times they were expected to run budget surpluses to reduce the debt. The Keynesian revolution that inverted the old-time fiscal religion allowed politicians to claim that budget deficits were required for fiscal responsibility, in contrast to the long-standing ethos that deficits in normal times were a sign of profligacy.

In their insightful treatment of the recent economic contraction in the United States, Charles Rowley and Nathanael Smith show that the consequences of the Keynesian inversion of the old-time fiscal religion are as deeply troubling as they are difficult to reverse. Despite the years of Thatcher and the years of Reagan, the intellectual climate of opinion is still highly collectivist. Rowley and Smith remind us that the Keynesian vision is still relevant to democratic politics. This vision holds that the only bad policy for a nation is *laissez faire*. Any policy is better than no policy, even though some policy measures might be regarded as better than others. Keynesian economics is a theory of market failure on a large scale, wherein any problem has a solution that runs through some government program.

If some people don't own homes, there can be a government program to increase ownership. If some people can't meet the financial terms necessary to secure home ownership, there can be a government program to subsidize such ownership. If such a program of subsidization requires businesses to offer imprudent loans, there can be government programs to guarantee the payment of such loans. And if the volume of such imprudent loans expands to gargantuan proportions, we enter into the new world of TARP, bailouts, and governmental appointment of corporate officers.

While Keynes favored the socialization of investment, I doubt if he would have favored such actions as these had he foreseen them. Keynes would not have thought such policies possible, because he believed that policy was effectively in the hands of a few wise men who would not be subject to what we now recognize as ordinary politics. Keynes viewed democratic outcomes as being moderated by the elitist presuppositions of Harvey Road, Cambridge, wherein a few wise men would pursue proper courses of action independent of electoral concerns.

Rowley and Smith remind us that democratic outcomes have little in common with the image of Harvey Road and instead conform far more closely to the Ancient Roman image of bread and circuses. As nearly any person will tell you, the best tax is one that someone else pays. Under the old-time religion of balanced budgets, bread and circuses could only be provided by imposing taxes. The Keynesian revolution countenanced the provision of bread and circuses through borrowing. While borrowing implies taxation in the future, the timing of periodic elections creates particularly short time horizons with respect to political action, leading to an internal dynamic that in the absence of suitable constitutional constraint continually pushes problems into the future for others to deal with.

In *Systems of Survival*, Jane Jacobs describes the character of flourishing societies as due to a perilous balance between what she describes as two distinct moral syndromes, the commercial and the guardian. A flourishing society needs both, but troubles and sorrows arise as the two syndromes and the people and offices that carry them come increasingly to commingle. The political logic of the Keynesian orientation promotes this commingling between commercial and guardian syndromes. Rowley and Smith set forth a positive program that would restore some reasonable separation between the spheres of operation for those syndromes. Rowley and Smith have reaffirmed Adam Smith's wisdom and have shown a difficult but passable path by which we can escape the *Road to Folly*, though they also recognize that to do so requires displays of wisdom and resolve that might be hard to find in a nation becoming increasingly surfeited on bread and circuses.

Holbert Harris Professor of Economics
George Mason University

About The Locke Institute

John Locke
(1632-1704)

Officers of The Locke Institute

General Director
Charles K. Rowley, Ph.D.

Program Director
James T. Bennett, Ph.D.

Director of Legal Studies
Amanda J. Owens, Esq., J.D.

Editorial Director
Gordon Tullock, J.D.

Financial Director
Robert S. Elgin, M.A.

Administrative Assistant
Marjorie I. Rowley

Founded in 1989, The Locke Institute is an independent, non-partisan, educational and research organization. The Institute is named for John Locke (1632 – 1704), philosopher and political theorist, who based his theory of society on natural law, which required that the ultimate source of political sovereignty was with the individual. Individuals are possessed of inalienable rights, variously described by Locke as "life, health, liberty and possession", or more directly, as "life, liberty and property". It is the function of the state to uphold these rights since individuals would not enter into a political society unless they trusted that the state would protect these very rights that they already hold in the state of nature.

The Locke Institute seeks to engender a greater understanding of the concept of natural rights, its implications for constitutional democracy and for economic organization in modern society. The Institute encourages high-quality research utilizing, in particular, modern theories of property rights, public choice, law-and-economics and the new institutional economics, as a basis for a more profound understanding of important and controversial issues in political economy. To this end, it commissions books, monographs and shorter studies involving substantive scholarship written for a wide audience, organizes major conferences on fundamental topics of political economy, and supports independent research. The Institute maintains a publishing relationship with Edward Elgar Publishing. It also publishes its own monograph series.

In order to maintain its independence, The Locke Institute accepts no government funding. Funding for the Institute is solicited from private foundations, corporations and individuals. In addition, the Institute raises funds from the sale of publications. The Institute is incorporated in the Commonwealth of Virginia, USA, and enjoys non-profit, tax exempt status under Section 501(c)3 of the United States Internal Revenue Code.

Academic Advisory Council of The Locke Institute

Richard A. Epstein (President)
Professor of Law, University of Chicago

Armen Alchian
Emeritus Professor of Economics, University of California at Los Angeles

Michael A. Crew
Professor of Economics, Rutgers University

Antony de Jasay
Janville, Paluel, France

Harold Demsetz
Emeritus Professor of Economics, University of Los Angeles

About The Locke Institute

William M. Landes
Professor of Economics, University of Chicago

Henry G. Manne
Emeritus Dean of the Law School, George Mason University

Professor Sir Alan Peacock
The David Hume Institute, Edinburgh, Scotland

Judge Richard A. Posner
U. S. Court of Appeals for the Seventh Circuit
Senior Lecturer in Law and Economics, University of Chicago

Robert D. Tollison
Professor of Economics, Clemson University

Gordon Tullock
Emeritus Distinguished Professor of Law and Economics, George Mason University

Officers of the Institute are listed above. Please direct all enquiries to the address listed below:

The Locke Institute
5188 Dungannon Road
Fairfax, Virginia 22030
USA
Tel: (703) 934-6934
Fax: (703) 934-6927
Email: crowley@gmu.edu
http://www.thelockeinstitute.org

About the IEA

The Institute is a research and educational charity (No. CC 235 351), limited by guarantee. Its mission is to improve understanding of the fundamental institutions of a free society by analysing and expounding the role of markets in solving economic and social problems.

The IEA achieves its mission by:

- a high-quality publishing programme
- conferences, seminars, lectures and other events
- outreach to school and college students
- brokering media introductions and appearances

The IEA, which was established in 1955 by the late Sir Antony Fisher, is an educational charity, not a political organisation. It is independent of any political party or group and does not carry on activities intended to affect support for any political party or candidate in any election or referendum, or at any other time. It is financed by sales of publications, conference fees and voluntary donations.

In addition to its main series of publications the IEA also publishes a quarterly journal, *Economic Affairs*.

The IEA is aided in its work by a distinguished international Academic Advisory Council and an eminent panel of Honorary Fellows. Together with other academics, they review prospective IEA publications, their comments being passed on anonymously to authors. All IEA papers are therefore subject to the same rigorous independent refereeing process as used by leading academic journals.

IEA publications enjoy widespread classroom use and course adoptions in schools and universities. They are also sold throughout the world and often translated/reprinted.

Since 1974 the IEA has helped to create a worldwide network of 100 similar institutions in over 70 countries. They are all independent but share the IEA's mission.

Views expressed in the IEA's publications are those of the authors, not those of the Institute (which has no corporate view), its Managing Trustees, Academic Advisory Council members or senior staff.

About the IEA

Members of the Institute's Academic Advisory Council, Honorary Fellows, Trustees and Staff are listed on the following page.

The Institute gratefully acknowledges financial support for its publications programme and other work from a generous benefaction by the late Alec and Beryl Warren.

The Institute of Economic Affairs
2 Lord North Street, Westminster, London SW1P 3LB
Tel: 020 7799 8900
Fax: 020 7799 2137
Email: iea@iea.org.uk
www.iea.org.uk